The Islamic Paradox

Shiite Clerics, Sunni Fundamentalists,
and the Coming of Arab Democracy

Reuel Marc Gerecht

The AEI Press

Publisher for the American Enterprise Institute

WASHINGTON, D.C.

Available in the United States from the AEI Press, c/o Client Distribution Services, 193 Edwards Drive, Jackson, TN 38301. To order, call toll free: 1-800-343-4499. Distributed outside the United States by arrangement with Eurospan, 3 Henrietta Street, London WC2E 8LU, England.

Library of Congress Cataloging-in-Publication Data
Gerecht, Reuel Marc
    The Islamic paradox : Shiite clerics, Sunni fundamentalists, and the coming of Arab democracy / Reuel Marc Gerecht.
    p. cm.
    Includes bibliographical references.
    ISBN 0-8447-7179-1 (pbk. : alk. paper)
    1. Middle East—Politics and government—20th century. 2. Islam and politics—Middle East. I. Title.

    DS62.8.G456 2004
    320.956'09'051—dc22

                                                              2004023389

10 09 08 07 06 05 04   1 2 3 4 5 6 7

Cover photograph caption: Shiites and Sunnis Unite to Oppose Occupation

Printed in the United States of America

Contents

The Islamic Paradox:
Shiite Clerics, Sunni Fundamentalists, and the Coming of Arab Democracy

Reuel Marc Gerecht

Is there an end to bin Ladenism? The wars on terrorism and in Iraq and Afghanistan could become futile endeavors if holy warriors endlessly regenerate themselves, drawing strength and new recruits from an ever-vibrant Muslim jihadist culture. September 11 propelled us massively into the Middle East. As American and foreign body counts mount in military actions abroad, spreading democracy in lands where the United States is increasingly unwelcome seems to many dangerously naïve. The Arab world appears to hate us as much as it ever did imperial Great Britain and France. Serious people in Washington talk about an expeditious withdrawal from Iraq. Prestigious think tanks plan departure scenarios and dilate on what went wrong. The Democratic nominee for president, Senator John Kerry, appears to view stability, not democracy, as the primary precondition for an American exit from Mesopotamia.[1] Even prowar Republicans have public doubts about the wisdom of the invasion.[2] In private, at Washington's working lunches and dinner parties, more and more people question—or forget—their approval of President George W. Bush's decision to topple Saddam Hussein. For many on the left and right, the Iraq war is disconnected from, indeed counterproductive to, the Bush administration's struggle against Islamic extremism and its hopes to see the region politically transformed.

1

Powerful historical forces at work in the United States and the Middle East will likely keep us in Iraq and Afghanistan and prevent both countries from descending into chaos. More important, they are likely to push the Muslim world toward democracy. But the confluence of these forces is not what the Bush administration expected when Abrams tanks crossed the Kuwaiti border. Americans, Shiite Muslim clerics, and Sunni Muslim fundamentalists have become the great actors of modern Middle Eastern history. Among them there is little mutual affection or admiration. They are certainly not of the same mind on the Iraq war and Washington's fight against Islamic holy-warrior terrorism. But the three together are the keys to spreading democracy throughout the greater Middle East. Shiite divines and Sunni fundamentalists are our salvation from future 9/11s.

The Bush administration, of course, does not yet see it that way. Neither do most Muslims. But, if we look at the United States post 9/11, Iraq's and Iran's Shiites, and Sunni Arabs elsewhere, it should not be hard to see why the coming of democracy to the Middle East is not just a dream of an American president who knows virtually nothing about the Muslim world. The United States and the two major branches of the Islamic faith, thanks to Osama bin Laden and Saddam Hussein, now have a common, if acrimonious, destiny.

The Americans

In the eyes of such influential historians as Princeton University's Bernard Lewis and Johns Hopkins University's Fouad Ajami, the Saudi holy warrior Osama bin Laden drove home a truth about the Muslim Middle East more painfully than the fallen shah of Iran and the generals of Algeria. Autocracy had fueled Islamic extremism. The jihadist spirit of 9/11 was born in Saudi Arabia, Egypt, and Pakistan, in an often turbulent marriage between dictators and Islamic fundamentalists in the 1970s and 1980s. Sometimes violently attacked, fundamentalists became heroes opposing tyrants. Often supported by the state, they were a loyal or tolerated "opposition," morally reinforcing the authority of conservative rulers while directing their society's frustrations outward toward Western enemies. For the radical who wanted to shatter the status quo, America was always the enabling power behind the ruler's despotism.[3]

Before the National Endowment for Democracy, a bipartisan grant-giving institution funded by the U.S. government to support the worldwide growth of democracy, President George W. Bush signaled that he saw this nexus between tyranny and Islamic extremism as *the* lesson of 9/11. Using liberal language that not even Jimmy Carter or Ronald Reagan, the twentieth century's most effective presidential advocates of human rights, ever directed toward the Middle East, President Bush took issue with the old European and modern American skepticism about the liberal possibilities of Muslim societies. The 1975 Helsinki Accords, which pledged both the West and the Eastern Bloc to respect "human rights and fundamental freedoms," is now widely viewed as a Trojan Horse that dissidents behind the Iron Curtain and their Western supporters used to weaken the Soviet empire. Yet President Gerald Ford never conceived of this declaration of basic rights as applicable to the United States's Muslim allies in the Middle East.[4] Although few American officials have ever been as direct as the diplomat-historian George Kennan, most before 9/11 certainly would have been sympathetic to his observation that there "is no reason to suppose that the attempt to develop and employ democratic institutions would be the best course for many . . . [non-European] peoples."[5]

Reinforcing this critique of democracy's limitations in the Muslim world were other powerful intellectual currents. Even though Americans usually flinch at the suggestion of French influence on their thoughts, *tier mondisme*, the French-born doctrine that non-Western cultures and states should not be judged by Western standards and should be free from foreign, especially American, intrusion, had also taken a firm hold in many quarters. This disposition melded well with a conservative American sensitivity about questioning the morality of foreign cultures defined by faith. Eight months after the fall of Baghdad, President Bush rejected the past and officially announced a new strategy for the Middle East that had been developing in the White House since the "Axis of Evil" speech on January 29, 2002.

> Sixty years of Western nations excusing and accommo-dating the lack of freedom in the Middle East did noth-ing to make us safe, because in the long run, stability cannot be purchased at the expense of liberty. As long as the Middle East remains a place where freedom does not flourish, it will remain a place of stagnation, resentment, and violence ready for export. And with the spread of weapons that can bring catastrophic harm to our country and to our friends, it would be reckless to accept the sta-tus quo. Therefore, the United States has adopted a new policy, a forward strategy of freedom in the Middle East. This strategy requires the same persistence, energy, and idealism we have shown before. And it will yield the same results. As in Europe, as in Asia, as in every region of the world, the advance of freedom leads to peace.[6]

And the practice of American diplomacy has changed. The State Department now publicly and, according to American diplomats, privately has become more vigorous in recommend-ing more open political systems to the region's unelected heads of state. The Broader Middle East and North Africa Initiative, a democracy-building project initially pushed by the National Security Council, is trying to grapple with the diplomatic and strategic difficulties of advancing democracy in an area where not a single Muslim ruler has been popularly elected. The initiative envisions a Euro-American effort to seed and protect liberal insti-tutions and principles—especially women's rights—throughout the Muslim world. This Helsinki-like project absorbed the State Department's Middle East Partnership Initiative, which seeks to promote programs on progressive family law, literacy, local governance, and women's rights, and the Middle East Free Trade Area, which hopes to use capitalism and commerce as engines for political liberalization.[7]

Outside government, the Democratic think tank par excellence, the Brookings Institution, invested heavily with the modernizing emir of Qatar in an annual U.S.-Islamic World Forum that seeks dialogue and common ground between America and Muslim moderates and progressives.[8] Former president Bill Clinton, at the forum in Doha in January 2004, counseled the leaders and intellectuals of the Muslim Middle East to no longer use the Israeli-Palestinian confrontation as a diversionary tactic to avoid backing political and economic reform.[9] This view, according to senior State Department officials, is now regularly reinforced by diplomats abroad and at Foggy Bottom, which has historically viewed the Israeli-Palestinian confrontation as the central issue for U.S. foreign policy in the Middle East. Daniel Benjamin and Steven Simon, the director and senior director for counterterrorism on the Clinton administration's National Security Council, the authors of perhaps the finest book on the rise of bin Laden, *The Age of Sacred Terror*, underscore the liberal internationalist view that "democratization, however hazardous and unpredictable the process may be, is the key to eliminating sacred terror in the long term."[10]

And the Middle East's rulers have certainly taken the American discussion seriously. Saudi Arabia's Crown Prince Abdallah started in June 2003 "National Dialogues" about the need for greater transparency in government and better communication between the rulers and the ruled. The first dialogue included the country's Shiite minority, who happen to live on top of most of Saudi Arabia's oil in the Eastern Province. The Shiite issue is extremely sensitive: The ultra-militant Wahhabi religious establishment, which has been the backbone of Saudi power since the eighteenth century, considers Shiites heretics. Until the early twentieth century, Wahhabi warriors pillaged Shiite towns in southern Iraq, raiding the region for the last time in 1922. When Ibn Sa'ud, the founder of the modern Sa'udi state, conquered the holy cities of Mecca and

Medina in 1925, ending centuries of rule by the Hashemite family, Ibn Sa'ud's troops destroyed sacred Shiite tombs. Crown Prince Abdullah's decision to include Shiites in the dialogues in 2003 was certainly made with an eye to neighboring Iraq, where a Shiite majority is on the verge of creating the first Arab Shiite-dominated state. Severe discriminatory actions against Shiites in the kingdom could well become heated topics of discussion in Iraq. As a senior Democratic congressional staffer who has long handled the Middle East remarked after visiting Saudi Arabia in January 2004, "the timing and seriousness of Saudi reform is unmistakably connected to American actions. President Bush has sparked what appears to be a serious debate inside Saudi society about more responsive and responsible government."[11]

And Egypt's president-for-life, Hosni Mubarak, made tours of Europe and the Middle East in February and March 2004 in an effort to preempt and circumvent America's democracy initiative.[12] The Arab League, which is based in Cairo and often functions as a bureau of the Egyptian foreign ministry, also tried to counter possible American actions. Its chief, the former Egyptian foreign minister Amr Moussa, always underscores a solution to the Israeli-Palestinian conflict as a required preface for any foreign discussion of democracy in the Arab world.[13] The league's aborted March 2004 summit in Tunis revealed serious differences among Arab rulers, especially about the desirability of *any* initiative advocating democratic change in the region. Tunisia's president-for-life, Zine el-Abidine ben Ali, pulled the plug on the discussion by having his officials surreally announce that the "summit meeting's final communiqué [needed] to be something of substance. Three hundred fifty million Arabs want a sense that the repression that scars their region is ending."[14]

One may legitimately wonder whether either Democrats or Republicans, too, *really* want to push human rights and democracy in the region. Understanding the nexus between 9/11 and tyranny is one thing, constantly cajoling and arm-twisting Middle Eastern dictators and kings to liberalize another. The menace of al Qaeda has substantially deepened the liaison relationships between the

Central Intelligence Agency and the security and intelligence services in the Muslim world, especially with those of Egypt, Saudi Arabia, and Pakistan, the three states whose domestic politics, religious organizations, and foreign policies were critical to the development of bin Laden's holy-warrior terrorism. The policy of rendition, where the United States sends suspected terrorists to allied Muslim states for "aggressive" questioning, which first started under the Clinton administration, has become integral to the CIA's counterterrorist modus operandi. The near-term threat of a terrorist strike can understandably seem more pressing than the long-term dangers of Muslim dictatorships. And the old "realist" view of the region—that Arab Muslims owing to culture, religion, and history are probably doomed to despotism—has hardly vanished in America's foreign-policy elites.

For example, the former counterterrorism czar Richard Clarke aggressively attacked the idea that changing the political culture of the Middle East is doable or even desirable, since it, like the war in Iraq, distracts us from the campaign against al Qaeda, which requires us to fortify our relationships with Muslim states.[15] President Jimmy Carter's former national security advisor Zbigniew Brzezinski, a prominent "realist," makes similar arguments against President Bush's new approach. Brzezinski sees Osama bin Laden and al Qaeda as isolated in time, products of the Soviet-Afghan war, not an evolving decades-old movement of Sunni militancy that has become ever more lethal and anti-Western under the Middle East's post–World War II dictatorships. Taking the dominant European view of the region, he sees the Israeli-Palestinian confrontation as the crux of America's bad reputation in the Muslim world and the principal spark to contemporary Islamic militancy. Voicing a preference for stable, friendly dictatorships in the Middle East over rapidly delivered American-born democracy, he counsels "it is essential that U.S. policymakers not be seduced by doctrinaire advocates of an externally imposed and impatient democratization."[16]

And America's most influential "realist," former secretary of state Henry Kissinger, also started expressing concerns that the

Bush administration's aspiration to expand democracy in the Middle East might be too eager. In European foreign-affairs conferences, he complains about the "Trotskyite" nature of American neoconservatives, whose zeal has exceeded their common sense. No doubt remembering the fall of the shah of Iran, he warns back home that "when democratization is pushed in a conceptual and political vacuum, the outcome is likely to be chaos or regimes inimical to our values and perhaps our security." Although a supporter of the Iraq war, Kissinger cautions that "to compress the [democratic] evolution of centuries into an appropriate time frame risks vast unintended consequences." Kissinger sees real democratic success in Iraq as dependent on "a secular middle class [which] can emerge strong enough to insist on full representative democracy."17

The fear of radical Islamic fundamentalism gaining power through the ballot box will undoubtedly grow stronger when the possibility of democracy in the Middle East seems closer. When senior American officials talk about "generational" change in the Middle East, that the Broader Middle East Initiative will engage us in a decades-long effort to contain and roll back Islamic militancy, they are also saying they have no immediate desire to overturn the status quo. The State Department intentionally designed the Middle East Partnership Initiative, which spent $29 million in 2002 and $100 million in 2003, to focus on small-scale nonthreatening programs that Arab governments de facto controlled.18 Even influential neoconservative advocates of democracy in Iraq may not like the idea so much if elections reduce the personal freedoms and professional opportunities for women, not at all an unlikely prospect since Iraqi society today, like most societies in the Middle East, is much more socially conservative than it was in 1968, when the Baath Party first came to power. Advancing democracy and women's rights may actually be at odds in much of the Muslim world, especially in Egypt where Islamic fundamentalists and religiously oriented associations dominate social life. It is worthwhile to recall that Algeria's Islamic Salvation Front, better known by its French initials, FIS, first came into prominence in December 1989, through organizing massive demonstrations against secularism and women's rights. In all probability, FIS would have won the legislative, if not presidential, elections in 1991 if Algeria's generals had not decided to cancel the process after Islamists won the first parliamentary round. The cancellation of elections provoked one of the worst bloodbaths any Middle Eastern country had seen since the merciless internal score settling after the extinction of *l'Algérie française* in 1962.

Women obviously play an enormous role in shaping the culture and practice of modern Western democracies. And it may well be true, as the former director of the State Department's Policy Planning Staff Richard Haass once wrote, that "patriarchal societies in which women play a subservient role to men are also societies in which men play subservient roles to other men, and meritocracy takes a back seat to connections and cronyism."[19] Bernard Lewis certainly thinks that the role of women in Western societies has been a significant factor in the progress gap between Western and Islamic civilizations in the modern age.[20] But democracy can obviously start and survive in societies where women are second-class political citizens and in their personal relationships with men, to brutalize Balzac a bit, are *instruments de plaisir et l'honneur et la vertu de la maison.* If this were not the case, Anglo-American, German, French, and Japanese democracies could never have developed.

On the American Left and Right, there is hope that "moderate Muslims," who believe in some, perhaps many, of the central tenets of modern Western civilization—greater separation of church and state, the rule of law, representative government, and women's rights—are a silent majority in the Islamic world, waiting to develop provided the Middle East's dictatorial regimes loosen their grip. With his regular references to the importance of "moderate Muslims" post 9/11, Deputy Secretary of Defense Paul Wolfowitz believes they are the missing link to a democratic dispensation in the Middle East.[21] For many American officials who supported the war in Iraq and for many Americans who did not but nevertheless now hope for the best, Iraq has become the great democratic experiment, where a secular, more-or-less liberal political system is supposed to serve as a beacon to the rest of the region. Neoconservatives inside the government and out advocated war against Saddam Hussein and early on threw their support behind Ahmad Chalabi, the head of the former exile group, the Iraqi National Congress, in large part because they believed the circumstances within Iraq (decades of hideous totalitarian rule) and Chalabi (a secular, liberal, but faithful Shiite) offered the possibility of a liberal democracy finally being born in a big, powerful Middle Eastern state.

But "moderate Muslims" may not be the key to a new, less-threatening Middle East. Odds are, they are not. Moderate Muslims, if defined by their attachment to secular culture or a certain affection for the United States, will probably lose ground as a democratic movement develops in the region. They are, simply, a minority. And Americans could certainly grow cold about spreading democracy in the Middle East if the victors do not at all look like us. Anyone who has a traditional Anglo-American understanding of democracy and its evolution—that democracy is primarily a means to liberal ends—instinctively recoils from the idea of empowering men of undeniably illiberal dispositions. Many might ask what is the point of a "forward strategy of freedom" if the beneficiaries use their liberty to excoriate the United States and Israel and possibly jack up the price of oil. Popularly elected governments always spend more on social programs than dictatorships, and oil is the Middle East's only cash crop.

And after Iraq, most Democrats and Republicans in Washington would strongly prefer not to further distance the United States from the Western Europeans, who do not care at all for the idea of forcefully pushing democracy in the Muslim world. The trans-Atlantic community is the bedrock of the American foreign-policy establishment. Many Europeans are concerned that political instability in the region—and pressuring the Middle East's dictatorships and kingdoms to reform could destabilize them— might lead to a new wave of Arab-Muslim refugees across the Mediterranean. Dictatorial regimes are more likely to restrict the travel of their citizens than democratic ones. France already has an Arab-Muslim minority that is at least 7 percent of its population. The suburbs and exurbs of many major cities, *les banlieues,* are overwhelmingly Muslim, and the growth within these communities of militant Islam has alarmed France's internal security service since the aftershocks of the Algerian civil war provoked immigrant and home-grown Muslim terrorism in the mid-1990s. (In 1995, a militant Muslim group under the guidance of the Algerian-born, French-educated Khaled Kelkal bombed the commuter rail system in Paris and attempted to blow a TGV high-speed train off its track.[22])

Fear of Muslim immigrants and Islamic militancy is no less vivid in the rest of Western Europe, where the Muslim percentage of the population keeps rising faster than the non-Muslim birthrate. The idea of spreading democracy in Arab lands is very likely to be seen at cross-purposes with Europe's increasing anxiety about its Muslim denizens. And after the March 11 bombings in Madrid and the fall of Spain's pro-American, prowar government, it is not unlikely that European governments will especially want to keep their distance from American endeavors that might further rattle the Middle East. The Euro-centric nature of America's foreign-policy professionals could easily diminish the scope, energy, and muscle of any pro-democracy initiative, which, if serious, would put an angrier Europe on the backburners of American foreign policy.

But the fear of 9/11, of another 9/11, will probably be sufficient to drive forward, however fitfully, nervously, and slowly, the current consensus in Washington that the politics of the Muslim Middle East must change. Even though Democratic and Republican foreign-policy circles disagree bitterly among themselves and with each other on whether the war in Iraq has helped or hurt America's battle against the holy-warrior terrorism of Osama bin Laden, neither side seems inclined yet to reject the nexus between tyranny and Islamic extremism. As the 9/11 Commission report reads, "Tolerance, the rule of law, political and economic openness, the extension of greater opportunities to women—these cures must come from within Muslim societies themselves. The United States must support such developments."[23]

And President Bush's still firm intention to establish democracy in Iraq will encourage the democratic ethic in America's policy

toward the entire region. Even if the president's realist-school sub-
ordinates at the State Department, the Pentagon, and the National
Security Council are less eager to advance prodemocracy initiatives
in the Middle East, presidential rhetoric drives foreign policy, at least
sufficiently to keep the bureaucracies from returning to a pre-9/11
world. Rapid prodemocracy change in Washington's approach to
the Middle East certainly is not imminent, but the direction of the
shift under President Bush seems irreversible. And even if Senator
John Kerry has suggested that stability, not democracy, is the more
practical objective of American forces in Iraq, it will be difficult for
the senator, if he is elected president in November, to leave the
country before it has a functioning democracy.

Establishing a democracy is actually the least dangerous
option for the United States. Although an increasing number of
voices, on the left and right, think that creating an "Iraqi strongman" would allow Washington to withdraw American troops—
and this was certainly a factor in national security advisor
Condoleezza Rice's and her deputy Robert Blackwill's enthusiastic
embrace of Iyad Allawi as the Iraqi prime minister—mechanically
this makes little sense. The resurrection of an effective Sunni/
former-Baathist-led Iraqi army has proven difficult. There may
not be that many former Baathist Sunni military officers who
want to pledge themselves to a new democratic order where they
will have to pummel Sunni insurrectionists, with whom they may
well share family ties, on behalf of a Shiite-led political order.
And the United States is probably lucky this has not happened,
since such an army could send the Shiites en masse into the
streets, particularly if such a force were recklessly deployed
against the armed young men following the radical young cleric,
Muqtada as-Sadr. The anti-American violence that we have seen
from the followers of Sadr would pale in comparison to the violence U.S. forces would encounter if the mainstream Shiite community actually believed America was abetting the return of a
Baathist, Sunni-led army.

Conversely, any attempt to create rapidly a Shiite-led force
without a parallel political process advancing an elected national

government would likely, as we will see, provoke Grand Ayatollah Sistani and the senior clergy of Najaf to call the Shiite community out against the Americans and the nonelected Iraqi government. Prime Minister Allawi, who grew to manhood among Sunni Baathists, may be willing to stand against the wishes of the traditional Shiite clergy, but he would likely not find many other prominent Shiites to join him. And either a Sunni or Shiite Arab dictatorship could provoke the Kurds to quit Iraq, an idea that already has appeal among the non-Arabic speaking young Kurds who have grown up since 1991 in Anglo-American-protected Iraqi Kurdistan. The Kurds, Turkey, Iran, the United States, and Iraq's Arabs could possibly confront each other over an independent Kurdistan. The Kurds are unlikely to divorce themselves from Iraq—they know well the precarious geopolitical and economic position they are in—but if one thing could make them take the jump it is the return of an Arab dictatorship to Baghdad. However difficult it may be to establish workable democratic procedures in Mesopotamia, trying to advance the re-creation of an army too quickly would probably force Washington to commit more troops, not fewer, to protect American and Iraqi lives. This is why Dr. Kissinger described democracy building as "the only exit strategy."24

Only a quick-withdrawal policy advanced by a determined Kerry administration, admittedly a possibility given Senator Kerry's deep-rooted Vietnam-era sensibilities, could shatter American perseverance. But Kerry would run against the 9/11 understanding widely held, if not publicly confessed to, by many of the Clintonites who would staff his administration. They know that running from Iraq—by declaring a victory over Saddam Hussein and getting out—would be seen throughout the Muslim Middle East as an enormous defeat for the United States. Bin Ladenism, which psychologically kicked into high gear after President Clinton's "Black Hawk Down" retreat from Somalia, could be supercharged by a rapid American departure. Kerry could certainly ignore the misgivings of the al Qaeda–savvy Clintonites, who are by and large deeply conflicted about the war (most appear to see it as a catalyst, not a partial antidote, to Islamic extremism). The Brzezinski analysis of Islamic terrorism—no nexus between Muslim dictatorships and anti-American Islamic extremism; the Israeli-Palestinian confrontation is the problem—could possibly gain ground, especially within a party addicted to the peace processing of Palestinian nationalist and religious aspirations. The heart and soul of the Democratic Party still remains wary of, if not allergic to, the sustained use of American power.

Yet the American death toll from the fighting in Iraq will probably remain too small to galvanize sufficiently the quick-exit impulse within a Kerry administration. And even if Kerry loves the idea of stability and an Iraqi "strongman" as much as some senior officials of the Bush National Security Council, the CIA, and the State Department, Prime Minister Iyad Allawi and the American military simply will not soon be capable of creating an Iraqi military able to stand against Muqtada as-Sadr's "Mahdi Army" or the better-trained Sunni guerrilla forces. The "toughness" and viability of Allawi is completely dependent on the United States. Only national elections in Iraq and the legitimacy that comes with them are likely to change the power dynamic sufficiently to allow for an accelerated American departure.

Fear of a deconstructing Iraq and bin Ladenism will likely ensure that the post-9/11 school of thought led by Lewis and Ajami, however battered by "realist" counterattacks, will continue to hold the high ground within the Democratic and Republican Parties. Middle Easterners themselves will also strengthen the antiauthoritarian case. It is difficult for Americans to turn a deaf ear to appeals for democracy. As liberal *Washington Post* columnist Jackson Diehl, who regularly writes on the Arab world, recently observed,

> The most underreported and encouraging story in the Middle East in the past year has been the emergence in public of homegrown civic movements demanding political change. Two years ago they were nonexistent or in jail. Now they are out in the open even in the most politically backward places in the region: Egypt,

Saudi Arabia, Syria. . . . These people weren't created by George W. Bush. They are the homegrown answer to a decadent political order. . . . But they will tell you frankly: The new U.S. democratization policy, far from being an unwanted imposition, has given them a voice, an audience and at least a partial shield against repression—three things they didn't have a year ago.[25]

The most prominent liberal dissident in the Arab world, the Egyptian Sa'ad Eddin Ibrahim, has been highlighting the internal forces working for real change in the Middle East. An increasingly united opposition is developing in Egypt, still the most consequential Arab country, where liberal secularists like Ibrahim are joining fundamentalists in demanding more representative government. The new Supreme Guide of the Muslim Brotherhood, the oldest and most influential fundamentalist organization in the world, allied his followers in March 2004 to a plan for substantive but gradual constitutional and political reform. President Mubarak has ignored them so far, as he has the Alexandria Declaration, which was written in March 2004 at a pan-Arab conference of nongovernmental organizations convened by the Harvard-educated director of the newly built Library of Alexandria, Ismail Serageldin. And as Ibrahim sarcastically noted, Arab rulers dismissed the United Nation's Arab Human Development Report of 2002, "as if it were about another region on another planet."[26] The report, signed by a number of prominent Arab intellectuals, is scathing about the lack of individual freedom, women's empowerment, and education in the Middle East.[27] It will be increasingly difficult for Washington to side with Mubarak or whoever succeeds the seventy-six-year-old dictator against Egyptian appeals to open the system.

And in Iran, the ideas of liberty and democracy have been gaining ground on theocracy ever since Ayatollah Ruhollah Khomeini died in 1989. Pro-American sentiment in the country has grown enormously: Even anti-American clerics, who are probably searching for a means to shore up their popularity, toy with the idea of having a national referendum about restoring diplomatic ties with the United States. The conservative routing of the reformist wing of the clerical establishment in the state-controlled "elections" in February 2004 is very unlikely to halt for long the great debates the Iranian people, and especially their clergy, have been having for one hundred years about constitutional government and democracy—debates often fueled by the Iranian and Arab Shiite clerics in Najaf, Iraq, the preeminent center of Shiite religious thought through much of the nineteenth and twentieth centuries.

If one has traveled in the Middle East since March 2003, if one listens to or reads the Arab and Iranian media, it is impossible not to see that all eyes are now on Iraq. Everybody wants to see whether in the end the United States will be laid low or emboldened. With hope and trepidation, they watch the Shiites, who, owing to America's invasion, have overturned the centuries-old Arab Sunni dominion. Given the Arab satellite-news coverage of the Sunni and Shiite "resistance" to the foreign invaders and the new Iraqi government, many in the Middle East probably believe the Americans are going down in defeat. The guerrilla violence of Sadr has already convinced many in the United States, and it would appear just about everyone in Europe, that a Shiite-led democracy is a dream. And if the United States were to withdraw precipitously, the ensuing power struggle could well lead to internecine strife where a Shiite military "strongman" would eventually claw his way to the top. The Broader Middle East Initiative is dead on arrival if the United States fails in Iraq, and the odds of a Middle Eastern "wave of democratization," to borrow from Harvard professor Samuel Huntington, will in all likelihood drop significantly, at least in the short term. As Huntington pointed out in his book about democratization in the twentieth century, *The Third Wave*, a correlation of forces has usually sparked successful democratic movements. And a key element has often been the magnetism or will of the United States.

For a variety of reasons, most unknown or underappreciated by even the most devout democracy advocates within the Bush administration, the Muslim Middle East now has a better chance of a widespread democratic takeoff than at any time since the 1940s, when the relatively liberal age at the end of European imperialism gave way to fascism, communism, and military autocracy. Post-Saddam Iraq is a microcosm of the opportunities and pitfalls for representative government in the region. The heroes or villains in this story will be Iraq's Shiites, particularly their senior clergy. Will they back democracy, or will they make another try at creating a theocratic Islamic-law state? Does the Bush administration understand Grand Ayatollah Ali Sistani, Iraq's preeminent Shiite divine, better than the Carter administration understood Iran's Grand Ayatollah Ruhollah Khomeini? In their differences and similarities, in the historical forces that produced them, lies the future of Iraq and the Middle East.

The Shiites

When the Coalition Provisional Authority (CPA), led by Ambassador L. Paul Bremer, first realized in the fall of 2003 that Shiite clerics would be the most important political players in American-occupied Iraq, it was not a happy discovery. American diplomats and spooks in Baghdad were used to dealing with highly Westernized Sunni Arab elites, or thoroughly secularized Iraqi Shiites in exile organizations like the Iraqi National Congress and the National Accord. Ditto for most journalists, who if they spent time in the Arab world usually did so in the company of Sunnis and Christians, the parents of modern Arab nationalism. The pan-Arab idea has never been friendly toward sectarian identities. And, face to face, Shiite Iraqi clerics often are little fun. They have generally far less personal warmth than their Sunni counterparts, who are more egalitarian and informal. Inclined to talk elliptically, when not dismissively, to foreigners and endowed with the hubris that comes easily to accomplished lawyers, the Shiite ulama have become for many U.S. officials enormously frustrating partners in rebuilding Iraq. They did not act according to plan, insisting on more democracy sooner than the Provisional Authority believed safe.

They resisted approving an interim constitution, the Transitional Administrative Law, that checks the superior power of the Shiite community at the ballot box, and now state they may not honor the document Shiite members of the interim Iraqi Governing Council signed.

Yet Iraq's Shiites and their clerics have probably become the most important players in modern Middle Eastern history. They, with their Shiite brethren in Iran, are on the cutting edge of permanently instilling the ideas of freedom and democracy into Muslim thought and political practice. Iraq's Shiites, especially the senior clerics residing in the shrine city of Najaf, who are not at all liberal democrats, will be the driving force behind any American success in Iraq and quite possibly "the forward strategy of freedom" beyond.[28] Indeed, precisely because Iraq's seminarians seek to blend politics and faith into a system where government is nevertheless clearly the servant of the commonweal, Iraq can serve as a catalyst for serious democratic change throughout the region.

Ayatollah Khomeini shook the Arab world with the Islamic revolution in 1979 and inspired radical Sunni Islamists to make a violent play for power. His antithesis, Najaf's Grand Ayatollah Sistani, could much more deeply influence grassroots Muslim religious organizations and fundamentalist political parties, on which depends the fate of democracy in the Middle East. Even though Arab and non-Arab Sunnis would be loath to accept the idea, their immediate political future is likely in the hands of those coreligionists they have belittled and usually oppressed for 1,300 years. And most American liberals and conservatives will strongly resist the idea that Islam's clergymen and lay fundamentalists, who usually dislike, if not detest, the United States, Israel, and progressive causes like women's rights, are the key to liberating the Muslim Middle East from its age-old reflexive hostility to the West. These men, not the much-admired liberal Muslim secularists who are always praised and sometimes defended by the American government and press, are the United States's most valuable potential democratic allies, assuming the Bush administration and the Shiite clerics first get it right in Iraq.

At least 60 percent of Iraq's population, the Shiite Arabs, like Iraq's Kurds, were severely oppressed by the country's modern, Sunni-Arab-dominated regimes. Unlike the Kurds, the Shiites and particularly their clergy have not been effusively thankful to the Americans for rescuing them from Saddam Hussein's Orwellian slaughterhouse. They have been slow to forgive the Americans for the "betrayal" (the ugly, oft-repeated word in Arabic is *khiyana*) following the first Gulf War, when U.S. forces stood idle in the southern Iraqi desert while Saddam put down the great rebellion that President George H. W. Bush had encouraged. Tens, perhaps hundreds, of thousands perished. Every senior cleric in Iraq has issued numerous *fatwas* (juridical opinions) on how to separate, bathe, bless, and rebury the bones of family members found in mass graves.

The renowned and late American diplomat Hume Horan, widely considered to be the finest Arabist since World War II, tried from May through November 2003 to develop a relationship with the four grand ayatollahs of Najaf, the most senior Shiite clergy in Iraq. He was ably seconded by Michael Gfoeller, an Arabic-speaking foreign-service officer mentored by Horan decades earlier in Saudi Arabia. A former student at Harvard of the great British orientalist Hamilton Gibb and by birth half Persian, Horan was the Provisional Authority's only all-purpose Arabist, a sixty-nine-year-old repository of Middle Eastern knowledge constantly called upon, sometimes for the most menial linguistic matters (I watched him receive the complaints of the female laundry crew of the Provisional Authority, who were being regularly searched by male American soldiers and denied regular bathroom breaks).

Horan, who preferred the company of Shiite to Sunni Iraqi clerics—discussions with the former "mercifully did not get stuck in the great dismal swamp of the Arab-Israeli question"[29]—eventually met three of the four grand ayatollahs. Horan actually scheduled a meeting with Sistani in August 2003, the only American official the grand ayatollah ever agreed to see, but the meeting did not happen, owing to mechanical difficulties with a helicopter assigned to transport the ambassador from Baghdad. The next day, on August 24, an attempt was made to assassinate Grand Ayatollah Muhammad Sayyid al-Hakim, and the atmosphere in Najaf changed. Seeing U.S. officials thereafter, according to Horan, could have made Sistani appear solicitous of American protection. A direct channel between the Grand Ayatollah and the Americans never developed.

Horan's clerical perseverance and knowledge of Islamic history unfortunately remained atypical among the State Department, CIA, and Pentagon civilian employees who were the brain center of the Provisional Authority. According to State Department and CIA officials, Ambassador Bremer in particular did not relish contact with Shiite clergymen. The National Security Council's Ambassador Robert Blackwill, the Iraq coordinator for the White House, had to politely read the riot act to Bremer in December 2003 to ensure that he did not confront Sistani over the now-aborted American plan to use caucuses to elect a provisional Iraqi government. Even though large street demonstrations and the rebellious actions of the Shiite members of the American-appointed Iraqi Governing Council taught the Bush administration and the Provisional Authority that they could not construct a democratic system ignoring Najaf's senior clergy, anticlerical sentiment among American officials remains strong.

No elder Arabist has yet replaced Horan, who left Iraq in November 2003 as an American intermediary to the senior clergy. Officials at Langley, Foggy Bottom, and on the NSC aggressively pushed the candidacy of the pro-Sunni Allawi for prime minister in part because he was not seen as close to the clergy. His organization, the Iraqi National Accord, has always been a refuge for former Baathist Sunni military officers and consequently had virtually no following among the Shia. Allawi is a secularized Shiite of no discernable religious education or affection, whom Ayatollah Sistani repeatedly refused to meet until the Iraqi Governing Council and the Bush administration chose him as prime minister. (Sistani acquiesced in Allawi's selection perhaps in part, as the Iraqi writer Kanan Makiya suggested, because he

was willing to see whether Allawi could corral the Sunni rejec-
tionists in central Iraq.30) Even among those American officials who
view Sistani as a stabilizing force in Iraq—the Grand Ayatollah
reached out to Sunni Arab clerics; worked against the anti-American
Shiite firebrand, Muqtada as-Sadr; and usually recommended coop-
eration, not confrontation, with the occupation—suspicions about
his political intentions abound.

Some wonder about his "Persianness." Sistani, like many clerics in Iraq, is Iranian by birth and early education. Iranian Shiism
was the catalyst for the Muslim world's only true Islamic revolution, and there is just something unsettling in many American
eyes—and in many secular Iraqi ones—with Persian mollahs,
even when they have spent nearly sixty years in Iraq. And, Sistani
has close family in Iran and could thus be subject to blackmail by
Tehran's ruling mollahs, who have a penchant for using family
coercion as a means of silencing its own clerical dissidents.
Further, some just do not believe that any accomplished Muslim
religious scholar, a *faqih*, can subordinate the Islamic Holy Law to
the ever-changing norms and dictates of democracy. Of the
dozens of American officials I spoke with in Washington and Iraq
since the fall of Saddam Hussein, only a few do not fear the Shia
and the fact that the future of Iraq, and the fate of Americans in
it, are so dependent on men who once a year may whip themselves with chains and swords to expiate their sins and express
their love of God. With the first national elections scheduled for
January 2005, Shiite religious parties soon will start aggressively
to seek followers and declare more concretely their principles. No
single party can now probably command the allegiance of a decisive bloc of votes. But, the more we know about them, the more
nervous we may become.

The best known of the Shiite organizations is the Supreme
Council for the Islamic Revolution in Iraq (SCIRI), led by Abd al-
Aziz al-Hakim, the brother of SCIRI's founder, the late Muhammad
Baqir, who was assassinated in August 2003 by a massive car
bombing in Najaf. Abd al-Aziz is a relative of Grand Ayatollah
Muhammad Sayyid al-Hakim, the second most influential cleric in

Iraq and the only grand ayatollah who is a full-blooded Iraqi Arab. He is the last of nine brothers: All but Muhammad Baqir perished under Saddam's regime.

Born in Iran in 1982 under the patronage of Ayatollah Khomeini, the SCIRI is the only Shiite group with a substantial, long-established, well-organized paramilitary force, the Badr Brigade, which numbers somewhere between 10,000 and 20,000 men (both U.S. and SCIRI officials give a regularly changing headcount). Man for man, the Badr is probably a vastly better fighting force than the "Mahdi army" of Muqtada as-Sadr. In Shiite neighborhoods and schools, members of the Badr have been harassing women to wear appropriately conservative clothing. It strongly appears that Iran has deployed a substantial number of officers from both the Revolutionary Guards Corps and the Iranian intelligence ministry among the tens of thousands of Iranian pilgrims who can freely cross the border to visit the holy shrine cities inside Iraq. According to both U.S. and Iraqi officials, individual members of the Badr Brigade have aided these Iranian officials with transportation, lodging, and other needs where a fluent command of Iraqi Arabic is required. Relatively few non-Arab Iranians, even among the clergy, speak Arabic well; a significant number of Iraqis, exiled to Iran during the Iran-Iraq war, speak Persian fluently. Until the fall of Saddam Hussein, the Badr was financially dependent on Iran. It is most unlikely the Badr and the SCIRI are now financially independent of Tehran. According to Iranian clerics, Iran's Revolutionary Guards Corps, the bulwark of clerical power in the Islamic Republic, still considers the Badr to be operationally integrated within the Guard Corps' command structure. Whether it still in fact is as an organization is an open question.

Another open question is Abd al-Aziz's real political preferences. He is reportedly as close to the Iranians as his assassinated brother; sympathetic to a political system where clerics are important, if not the dominant, actors; and often zealously critical of American "failures" in Iraq (after his brother was slain Abd al-Aziz declared that "Iraq must not remain occupied and the occupation must leave so that we can build Iraq as God wants us to do").[31] Yet when Abd al-Aziz visited Washington in late January 2004, he made a personal plea in a private meeting with President Bush for the Americans to persevere in the country. He is described by Horan as "not a natural enemy" of the Americans, who is "an asset for all we and good Iraqis want."[32] But Horan did not find Abd al-Aziz "naturally cut out to be a leader in a politically turbulent situation."[33] He often seemed indecisive and "does not project the confidence that the big clergy do."[34]

Odds are Abd al-Aziz and the SCIRI will not make a play for the country's secular, highly Westernized Shiites, who are numerous though unorganized. It just is not a natural fit, even though Abd al-Aziz's actions have been more moderate than his rhetoric. More likely, the SCIRI will acquire an increasingly anti-American discourse as it tries to attract religiously oriented Shiites, who might be inclined to vote for the radical movement behind Muqtada as-Sadr, who is from Iraq's most famous and revolutionary clerical family. Sadr has yet to create an official party to incorporate the militant young men called the *Sadriyyin*, named after his father, Grand Ayatollah Muhammad Sadeq as-Sadr, who audaciously preached against Saddam and was murdered in 1999. The young Sadr's strongholds are in the poor Shiite slums of Baghdad and Basra, although he appears to be drawing numerous recruits from mid-size towns, like Kut and Nasiriyya, throughout the country's Shiite regions. He, too, has undoubtedly received Iranian aid. His street-power persona among Iraq's poor, young Shiite men is appealing to the revolutionary hard-core in the Islamic Republic. Sadr has received favorable coverage in the Iranian press aligned with Iran's clerical leader, Ali Khameneh'i, and the Revolutionary Guards Corps, the bulwark of clerical power and a virtual mini-state within Iran. The Guards Corps appears to be the dominant Iranian player within Iraq.

With the exception of Sistani and possibly Grand Ayatollah Muhammad Sayyid al-Hakim, Sadr is the only Shiite with a solid, national political base faithful to him. Guessing reliably the percentage of Shiites loyal to Sadr is difficult. Guessing the percentage of his followers who would remain loyal to him if he were to oppose a democratic process already under way with elections is even more precarious. It is a decent bet that Sadr's sympathizers today account for around 10 or 15 percent of the country's Shiites. Ahmad Chalabi, the leader of the Iraqi National Congress who dominated the Iraqi Governing Council until Ambassadors Bremer and Blackwill downed him, has repeatedly tried to bring the *Sadriyyin* into the Shiite mainstream. He is unlikely to be successful. So far, these young men have not shown any appreciation for the more moderate politics of their elders. By taking Najaf, the shrine of Ali, and making a serious play for the control and finances of important urban mosques throughout Iraq, Sadr has belittled the authority of Sistani and the traditional clergy and thumbed his nose at the Shiite Council, a new informal political body representing both religious and secular Shiites. The council could become a significant political force in Iraq, especially if the Shiites feel compelled to vote as a bloc.

As in Iran at the dawn of the Islamic revolution, where young men were indispensable to Ayatollah Khomeini's efforts to intimidate Iran's senior traditional clergy, the *Sadriyyin* are the key to convulsing Iraq's accepted mores and loyalties. Sistani's massive march on Najaf after his return from medical care in London in August 2004, which forced Sadr to return the town and the Imam Ali shrine to the denizens of Najaf, is unlikely to end Sadr's challenge to the traditional clergy. Yet if Chalabi were to continue where Sistani left off and neutralize the *Sadriyyin* through politics and diplomacy, he would immediately become a significant national political force. In recognition of his achievement, urban moderate Shiites, who fear Sadr but do not want to see the Shiite community engaged in internecine strife, could well back Chalabi for national office. The established clergy, which has been suspicious of Chalabi, could also throw support behind the Iraqi National Congress (INC). If Chalabi or other Shiite politicians can outplay Allawi with Sadr and his followers, then the prime minister, who continues to have little solid support within the

Shiite community, could find himself without any future once elections, and not U.S. officials, become the decisive factor in Iraqi politics.

Even if Grand Ayatollah Sistani's truce and amnesty for Sadr and his followers hold and the young cleric survives the intermittent American manhunt and those within the Shiite community who wish him dead or exiled (many senior Shiite clerics view him as the gravest threat to the traditional clergy), he personally may not lead a radical Islamic movement in future elections. He would probably consider such politicking to be beneath his family's august bloodline. He has so far given little indication that he considers political compromise a long-term virtue. Nonetheless, it is possible that Sadr could turn himself into a politician, responsive to the electoral wishes of his community. Known for his love of food, Sadr lacks the waistline of a die-hard holy warrior. He could have enjoyed a martyr's death against American troops several times, yet he chose not to. Given his retreat from Najaf in August 2004, he certainly realizes that he cannot provoke the Shiite community into rebellion on his side. Nor can he put as many followers into the streets as Sistani—at this time probably the only fairly reliable barometer of future loyalty at the voting urns. Regardless of what happens to Sadr, his movement of young men is unlikely to disappear as an important political force. Although Sadr may try to form a party that he de facto controls, participation in a political process may prove unmanageable for such a revolutionary. The young men who follow or admire Sadr may be forced to go elsewhere, most likely to either an increasingly radicalized SCIRI or, more likely, to the oldest and most hard-core Islamic militant movement, the *Da'wa al-Islamiyya* ("the Islamic Call") Party.

Founded in 1967 and considered to be the oldest Shiite political organization in Iraq, the Da'wa is a fractious collection of Islamic activists, with multiple leaders and spiritual guides. The party recognizes Grand Ayatollah Sistani to be the preeminent cleric, but it has never been an organization best defined by its clerical allegiances or members. Like the *Sadriyyin*, Da'wa members are not above questioning Sistani's Iraqi credentials because of his Iranian blood. The organization cut its teeth in the 1960s and 1970s, recruiting Shiites from the neighborhoods that empowered the Iraqi Communist Party, which from the 1940s to 1960s was the most attractive political organization among Shiites.[35] Although brutally suppressed by Saddam Hussein, the Da'wa was the only organization to maintain active cells in southern Iraq capable of consistently evading Saddam's secret police and on occasion lethally striking against the regime.

Still militant and straightforward about their intentions and hopes to establish an Islamic government, the mid-level clerics and lay fundamentalists who are the soul and footsoldiers of the Da'wa are easily the most Leninist in manner and mien of Iraq's major parties. At higher levels, however, the Da'wa was supportive of the Coalition Provisional Authority. Ibrahim Ja'afari, a Da'wa leader and member of the Iraqi Governing Council, has often arranged the most sensitive communications between the Americans and the senior clergy in Najaf. According to American officials in Iraq, his information on the inner workings of the Shiite clergy and community has been among the most valued by the State Department and the CIA. Pierre-Jean Luizard, France's finest scholar on Iraq and the author of the best book on the Iraqi Shia, *La Formation de l'Irak Contemporain*,[36] thinks the Da'wa will probably play a double game (*"poker menteur"*), where the members nominally work with the American-led reconstruction while attacking it and its Iraqi allies from the outside. In Luizard's view, the Da'wa, like the *Sadriyyin*, could easily support armed struggle against the Americans.[37]

The SCIRI, the Da'wa, the *Sadriyyin*, and other explicitly religious Shiite political groups all declared that they are operating with the blessing and guidance of Grand Ayatollah Sistani. This is not true, but the clerical politics could become devilishly difficult for the American embassy in Baghdad to figure out, particularly since Sistani will likely continue to refuse direct contact with U.S. officials. And indirect communication with the senior clergy, especially after the departure of Ambassador Horan, greatly complicated the work and understanding of the Coalition Provisional Authority, which largely became dependent on representatives of the SCIRI, the Da'wa, and the Iraqi National Congress for messages to and from the grand ayatollah. The American embassy in Baghdad, already more bureaucratic in its internal structure than the CPA and equally fearful of deploying personnel outside of highly guarded compounds, could become even less informed about the Shiite community and its divines. And Sistani and the traditional clergy will probably remain indirect about their preferences within the Shiite community. Although the senior traditional clerics loath Sadr, they do not like moving against radicals. According to religious scholars close to Sistani, the grand ayatollah hates violence. By personality and training, he is a consensual cleric—the opposite of Khomeini—who will try to maintain as much fraternity as possible within the Iraqi Shiite community. Historically, the Shiites have often split along ideological, family, and personal lines, much to the advantage of their Ottoman, British, and Arab Sunni overlords. And Sistani may not back off his demand that the Transitional Administrative Law be rewritten so that neither the Arab Sunnis nor Kurds can block the adoption of a new constitution. Once electoral politics start to roll in Iraq—and the violence in the Sunni triangle is unlikely to delay for long the timetable for constituent and parliamentary elections nationwide—the grand ayatollah could appear to Washington as the maestro of an increasing anti-American, anti-Iyad Allawi Iraq.

But we should not have an inordinate fear of anti-Americanism among the Shiites or think less of Sistani if he refuses the American-approved interim constitution or obstructs the new Iraqi government. His actions may confound the Bush administration's timetable for Iraq. They may spark again large street protests, which could turn violent. But they certainly will reveal that this cleric and those who follow him are not cut from the same theocratic cloth as Khomeini. The course of Shiite history is now on Sistani's (not Sadr's) side, leading the faithful to an increasingly democratic understanding of Muslim mores.

Of course, an American visitor to Najaf, the center of Shiism in Iraq, could understandably conclude that the United States's fate is in the hands of medievalists. Shiite history can appear like a bizarre voyage, with few modern touchstones capable of sustaining democracy. This view is not uncommon among many Iraqis, even Shiites, who grew up in Baghdad, where the faith has been cantonized. Walk into the predominately Shiite, middle-class neighborhood of Karada, where lightly or unveiled Shiite women and their mates walk hand in hand, and you rarely see awkward tense glances between Muslims and unbelievers. Tolerance is tangible. In Najaf, however, the faith envelops you. For an unbeliever, it feels heavy and claustrophobic.

On the edge of a desert, fed only in modern times by a canal, Najaf is parched and plain. Two-story plaster and concrete houses compose most of its historic quarters. The palm trees, grass, and mud of the Tigris and Euphrates Rivers, the double spine of Mesopotamian civilization, are nowhere to be found. The city's largest open square is a sprawl of dirty khaki-colored tents. There are no *suq* smells of spices, leather, or carpets. No sounds of Western and Arabesque music. Pilgrimage trinkets, small household appliances, cheap clothes, Qur'ans, religious commentaries, and other necessities of daily life are sold and resold to the natives and religious pilgrims. From early morning until late at night, pedestrians and cars clog the streets. Even among the most devout, Najaf is known as the "village of Volvos." Saddam Hussein flooded the town with the model 240 during the 1980–88 Iran-Iraq War to buy the loyalty of Shiites, who made up the bulk of his Sunni-led army. Traffic jams in Najaf are Volvo junkyards. And everywhere through the fumes, one sniffs the flow of corpses. From the golden-domed shrine of the caliph Ali, where the faithful carry, bless, and commend their deceased loved ones, to the town's enormous graveyards, where hundreds of thousands of lucky Shiites have been buried for centuries, a pilgrimage for the dead endlessly repeats itself.

Away from the smell and noise, inside Najaf's Imam Ali library (a three-story modern building recessed into a narrow winding street of row houses), Shiite history is stacked. With 600,000 volumes and 15,000 titles, it is the largest religious library in Iraq, the only great Shiite collection not destroyed by Saddam after the rebellion of 1991. In the floor-to-ceiling foyer wrapped with books, the librarians and clerics quickly take a visitor through time. In addition to the dead, students from all over the Muslim world have come to Najaf since the eleventh century, when its first religious school, or *madrasa*, opened. Although not always the preeminent center of Shiite learning—neighboring Karbala, the northern Iraqi town of Samarra, Isfahan, the capital of Persia's Safavid shahs, Tehran and the nearby older city of Ray, and the Iranian desert town of Qom have at times all vied for leadership—Najaf has always spiritually had a trump card as the burial site of Ali ibn Abi-Talib, the last of the four Arabian caliphs who oversaw the Muslim conquest of the Near East.

A cousin and son-in-law of the Prophet Muhammad, Ali is the father of the bloodline of all the *imams* who form the family tree of Shiite Islam. Shiism, or as it was first known, the *shi'atu Ali*, "the party of Ali," is in great part about the charisma that resides in divinely inspired men. The most charismatic of all are the male descendents of the Prophet via his daughter Fatima, the wife of Ali. Sunnis, who take their name from the phrase *sunnatu an-Nabi*, "the traditions of the Prophet," are about 85 or 90 percent of all Muslims. They, too, respect, even revere, Muhammad's lineage. But they have recognized the legitimacy of Islam's many caliphs, sultans, and amirs—in modern times, its colonels, generals, and presidents-for-life—irrespective of direct family ties to the Prophet. From the beginning, Sunni Islam has been wedded to the state, to the realities and compromises of power.

Shiism, though, is a faith forged overwhelmingly by adversity and defeat. The first great Sunni dynasty, the Umayyads of Damascus, fatally weakened Ali and killed his son Hussein, the most tragic of Shiism's many martyrs, on the plains of Karbala in 680. The second Sunni dynasty, the Abbasids, rode to power in 750 on propaganda playing to widespread Shiite sentiments. Once in power, however, the Abbasid caliphs in Baghdad firmly embraced Sunni orthodoxy. By the end of Islam's classical age in the ninth century, Shiism's would-be philosopher-kings, the *imams,* after the Caliph Ali, never commanded a land or army.

Shiism on occasion would be electrified by its own sectarian splits and mystical missionary movements. Great Shiite dynasties would arise. The Fatamids stormed out of North Africa in the tenth century, conquered Egypt, made the new city of Cairo into an intellectually vibrant metropolis, and briefly threatened the Abbasids with clandestine missionaries and armies before Saladin, the Sunni foe of Richard the Lionhearted, extinguished them. An offshoot of the Fatamids, the Assassins, would introduce organized political murder into the vocabulary of both the Islamic and Christian worlds. Another offshoot would produce the secretive Druze in Lebanon and still another the equally clannish and heretical Alawis, who today rule Syria. The Safavid shahs of the sixteenth century permanently married the Iranian identity and language with Shiism, threatened the Sunni Ottoman empire with fearless Sufi holy warriors, and built Isfahan into perhaps the most beautiful, certainly the most sensuous, city in the Islamic world. And the softer side of Iranian Shiism in the nineteenth century produced Bahaism, which is viewed by its followers and Muslims as a new religion and not a heretical sect. All the great revolutionary clerics of the twentieth century—Ruhollah Khomeini, the Iraqi Muhammad Baqir as-Sadr, and Muhammad Hussein Fadlallah of Lebanon—tried to convert Shiism into a faith of victors, to make Shiites act like Sunnis. The martyrdom of Ali's son Hussein, who marched with only a few followers against the Umayyads and toward a certain death, became for these men and their followers a symbol of revolutionary protest, not a Christ-like figure teaching in defeat the virtues of sacrifice and the ugliness of political power.

But traditional Shiism could never really revel in the glories of its empires or in its holy men who acted like princes. It was, at heart, uncomfortable with caesaropapism and theocracy. It was, however, increasingly identified with a body of religious scholars who carried forth the traditions and law of the Shiite community.

Over time, a small slice of the charisma that belonged to the twelve imams of the Alid line—the last of the twelve, Muhammad al-Mahdi, went into "hiding" in 874 near Samarra and will at the end of time return as the messiah—devolved onto the most accomplished members of the Shiite clergy. Because of their years devoted to studying the Holy Law, they became, at least in their own eyes if not always in the eyes of the faithful, "the representatives of the Hidden Imam."

Westerners who have forgotten how hard their Christian forebearers worked to deploy reason to defend their faith can have great difficulty understanding the mind and manners of clerics. In Najaf's madrasas, the students and the senior clergy, known collectively as the *Hawza,* learn a classical curriculum similar to the Latin trivium of a medieval European university. Whether followers of the theocratic creed of Khomeini or the more politics-averse, waiting-for-the-messiah faith of traditional seminarians, the Shiite ulama know they possess sufficient knowledge of the Holy Law, the *Shari'a,* to discern the most moral path for believers. They have given their lives to hone their reason, the most esteemed attribute among Muslim clerics, to fairly serve as ethical intermediaries between God and man.

Izz ad-Din al-Hakim, the youngest son of Grand Ayatollah Muhammad Sayyid al-Hakim, guided me through Najaf's twisting walkways to the exile home of Khomeini. It was an old, unpainted, sand-scratched wooden house with small barred windows. So far as Izz ad-Din knew, Iranian Shiite pilgrims, who almost immediately after the fall of Saddam Hussein in April started arriving in the holy cities of Najaf and Karbala in great numbers, were not visiting the ayatollah's former residence. Khomeini had lived in Najaf from 1964 to 1978, when the shah unwisely asked Saddam to boot the cleric from the country. Najaf was too close for comfort for Mohammad Reza Pahlavi, who feared the ayatollah's cross-border, clandestine clerical networking. In a Paris suburb, no longer under Iraqi surveillance, Khomeini and his lieutenants let loose a torrent of antishah propaganda via radio, cassette, telephone, and fax.

In Najaf, however, Khomeini perfected his political theory of a cleric-led Islamic revolution. It was a brilliant innovation, transforming the privileged position of Shiite clerics into an organized vanguard propelling the masses into the streets. Even though Khomeini had hoped that an Islamic revolution would spread throughout the Middle East, the Arab Sunni world was not captured by his call to arms against the region's U.S.-backed kings and dictators. Although fascinated by Khomeini's success—the Sunni Muslim Brotherhood, the mother of all Sunni fundamentalist movements, dreamed of toppling unrighteous Muslim rulers decades earlier—Sunni militants could not forgive Khomeini's allusions to the "Hidden Imam" and the suggestion that his authority and title (Khomeini was always called the *Imam* in Iran) was somehow supernaturally charged. The great divide in Islamic civilization, between the Sunnis and the Shiites, who predominate only in Iran, Iraq, and Lebanon, held firm.

"Khomeini was a great man," Izz ad-Din said evenly. "He triumphed over the shah, who was not a good man to his people. But Khomeini is the past. His way is not the future of Iraq."[38] Shaykh Muhammad al-Haqqani, a senior cleric close to Sistani, put it another way, "We want a non-Islamic government that is respectful of Islam." A highly respected teacher in Najaf, of Iranian descent and happy to guide a stranger through his impeccably clean, two-story religious school, Haqqani invited me and Iraqi and Iranian clerics to sit for a spread of lamb, chicken, and river fish. "There is a serious discussion of the Islamic Republic and the idea of Islam in Iraq. After Saddam, there is a strong desire to have more Islam here. We will not be Turkey. The Turkish Republic is offensive to the idea of Islam. However, very few people want to see an Islamic revolution and the *velayat-e faqih* [Iran's "rule of the jurisconsult"]. There is no strong desire here to copy the Islamic Republic."[39]

Slightly annoyed by my continuing questions about Khomeinism in Iraq, he tried again to explain. "If you want to do Khomeini self-study in Najaf, you are free to do so. His writings are available here. If you *can* find disciples of Khomeini, you are free to study with them. But if a student becomes too engaged in social affairs—for example, in the affairs of Muqtada as-Sadr—this student may not have time to study and advance through the system. This student should leave."[40] The Iranian clerics nearby nodded firmly.

Izz ad-Din and Haqqani are good examples of the Shiite clergy throughout Iraq. Both men appeared to be sincerely respectful, though not approving, of Najaf's most famous teacher. Khomeini had done what many religious scholars through the centuries had dreamed of. He downed a tyrant. Sunni and Shiite theologians have regularly discussed the idea of legitimate rule; the discussion is common because reality often fails minimum expectations. All of his abuses aside, and the Iraqi and Iranian Shiite clergy in Iraq are not hesitant to discuss Khomeini's awful errors, the founder of the Islamic Republic had shown that a king could be called to account. The idea of justice—that all men, be they of noble or humble birth, ought to live according to the same law—is resilient through Islamic history. Khomeini may himself have become a tyrant and betrayed his own obligation to live under law, but he did for one amazing moment, in the eyes of even politically adverse clerics who are repelled by Khomeini's hubris and rhetoric, render justice.

And the commentary on Khomeini that I often heard proved that the Iraqi clerical community had not been lost in a time-lag under Saddam Hussein. Even before the murder of Ayatollah Muhammad Baqir as-Sadr in April 1980, the Baathist regime had worked to isolate and psychologically undermine the Shiite religious establishment. After Sadr's death and the beginning of the 1980–88 war with Iran, an army of spies descended on the 'Atabat, the shrine cities that are the "doorways" to heaven for Shiites. According to Haqqani, at least 30 percent of the religious students in Najaf in the 1990s were moles. And the percentage could have been vastly greater. Clerics, too, were co-opted. Najaf, which had at least nineteen religious schools at the beginning of the twentieth century and was described as "the receiver of all the news of the world," turned inward and almost stopped functioning. The famous bookstores along al-Mutannabi street went *samizdat* and scrounged for paper. Overseas travel and communication of Shiite clerics were severely restricted and monitored. The always important ties between Najaf and Qom in Iran were nearly severed.

But, politically, most of Iraq's clerics empathically do not appear retrograde: They are not innocently itching to implement their own revolutionary designs, advancing and refining those of Khomeini or his Iraqi counterpart, the more intellectually gifted Muhammad Baqir as-Sadr, whose books—*Falsafatuna* (Our Philosophy) and *Iqtisaduna* (Our Economy)—laid the groundwork in the 1960s for a militant Shiite renaissance. In Najaf today, it is easy to find Sadr's works, as it is Khomeini's all-important *Hokumat-e Eslami* (Islamic Government), first compiled from the ayatollah's Najaf lectures in 1970, or political pamphlets of Khomeini's less-accomplished successor, Ali Khameneh'i. I could find no single cleric under the age of sixty who was not conversant with the works of Sadr and Khomeini and other key radical figures.

Yet, by and large, today's clergy views the great works of modern Shiite thought as outdated. *Falsafatuna*'s principal revolutionary theme is that Islam is a self-contained ideological system that rejects both communism and capitalism as foreign ideologies based on godless materialism. Sadr's third-way approach, which has many parallels among influential Sunni activists and which Khomeini later made famous in his revolutionary reproach, "Neither East, nor West," seems to have no serious following today among Iraqi Shiites, except among a homegrown militant minority, most notably among the *Sadriyyin*, and the expatriate hard core nurtured in Iran. This is not, as has been often suggested by secularized exiles, because the Iraqi clergy are following a quietist tradition, which views politics as spiritually polluting and best avoided. Far too much has been made about the politically adverse nature of the traditional Shiite clergy. Khomeini's revolutionary achievement, converting clerics into dictatorial politicians, was a logical, though hardly inevitable, extension of the traditional Shiite understanding that senior ulama, owing to their decades of learning, should advise shahs or prime ministers on the morality and legality of laws. Great traditional clerics of the twentieth century—the Iranians Abd al-Karim Ha'eri Yazdi, Mohammad Hosein Borujerdi, and Kazem Shariatmadari or the Iraqi Abu al-Qasim al-Kho'i, who probably produced more clerics than any other twentieth-century Shiite teacher—did not like to mix politics and religion. However, it is by no means clear that, if they had lived under democratic governments, these religious scholars would not have become more politically active.

The defining moment of modern Shiite thought, Iran's Constitutional Revolution of 1905–11, catapulted Shiite clerics into the modern age. By the turn of the twentieth century, an organized, hierarchical system of *mujtahids*, senior clerics capable of issuing their own juridical opinions, had crystallized. The ideas of modernist Shiite and Sunni Islamic thinkers also became known in clerical schools: men like Jamal ad-Din al-Afghani, Muhammad Abduh, and Rashid Rida, who reanimated Islamic pride through merging the Western belief in patriotism and progress with the traditional love and defense of the *umma*, the borderless community of all Muslims. Thereafter, Islamic rulers became much more subject to achievement tests. As the scholar Yitzak Nakash pointed out in *The Shi'is of Iraq*, "the Iranian Constitutional Revolution of 1905–11 provided the mujtahids [of both Iran and Iraq] with a vision of what an Islamic government should be."[41] In opposing the despotic actions of an Iranian shah, senior clerics saw themselves ideally as a supervisory body to a secular government. The legitimacy of a king's actions, indeed his very rule, could be dependent on the blessing of senior clerics. Khomeini grew directly from this tradition. So, too, has Sistani. Today in Iraq, it is a good bet that most Shiite clerics are political. After decades of unspeakable tyranny, they believe that clerics must watch over the political system to ensure that their flock is never again slaughtered.

But what is essential to understand is that the ideas of political legitimacy and justice have changed. They have been decisively and irreversibly secularized. The clerical movement in Iraq and Iran behind the 1905–11 revolution viewed constitutionalism as a means to buttress the Holy Law, which was the ultimate authority above ruler and ruled. In the clerical debates at that time, there was little to no room for the idea of democracy. The clerics who wanted to overthrow the Iranian shah, Mozaffar ad-Din, did not want to overthrow monarchy. The title of the most famous and galvanizing clerical tract in favor of the constitutional revolution, Muhammad Husayn Na'ini's *The Awakening of the Islamic Community and the Purification of the Islamic Creed,* gives a good idea of the centrality of Islam and the Holy Law to clerical constitutional politics. Compare that with the following fatwa of Sistani explicitly in favor of democracy. This is the opinion that unraveled America's postwar, go-slow planning and eventually led the Bush administration to seek help from the United Nations.

> The Occupational Authority in no way has the authority to choose members for the drafting committee of a Basic Law. In no way does any authority exist for such a drafting committee to represent the lofty interests of the Iraqi people or to translate into law the wishes and basic identity of the Iraqi people, the pillars of which are the glorious faith of Islam and society's values. The current [American] plan discussed is fundamentally unacceptable.
>
> Accordingly, popular elections are necessary so that each Iraqi who is of voting age can choose his representative for a constituent assembly. And then any Basic Law written by this assembly must be approved by a national referendum. It is incumbent upon all believers with their utmost commitment to demand this, and asserting the truth of this path is the best way that they can participate in this process.[42]

In the history of Islam, this opinion is revolutionary, equal to Khomeini's assertion of clerical supremacy. There is little reference in this judgment, which was issued on June 28, 2003, to Islam, and what reference there is, for a senior cleric who has devoted his life to the study of Islamic law, verges on the pro forma. It makes no allusion to any duties that man owes to God (*huquq Allah*), the common theme of both traditional and modern fundamentalist thought. Sistani is talking about inalienable rights that Muslims possess. In its essentials—one man, one vote and the moral obligation to have a constitution written by elected representatives and then approved by popular referendum—the fatwa is flawlessly secular, clearly and concisely asserting the people as the final political arbiter. Sistani's opinion is striking when compared to Khomeini's antidemocratic statements and actions before and after the revolution. The Princeton historian L. Carl Brown has well described Khomeini's vision, which married the Qur'anic conception of an absolute God with absolutist clerics.

> That political agenda can be simply stated: Islam provides a comprehensive sociopolitical system valid for all time and place. Thus, God is the sole legislator. Government is mandated in order to implement God's plan in this world. The only acceptable form of this Islamic government is that directed by the most religiously learned. This is the guardianship of the faqih (velayat-e faqih). Thus monarchy or for that matter any other form of government is unacceptable.[43]

Once in power, Khomeini and his clerical cohorts accordingly gutted the Iranian constitution, initially drafted by pro-revolution liberals, of any meaningful commitment to democracy. The idea that each Iranian would have had the right to select his or her representative to a constitutional convention would have been seen and denounced as an anti-Islamic plot.

Even though more than a few Western observers see in Ayatollah Sistani and the rise of his power vis-à-vis the Coalition Provisional Authority the beginnings of an Iraqi theocratic state, this description makes no sense. Sistani has done what Iran's prodemocracy dissident clerics have dreamed of doing: He has taken the all-critical moral imperative in Islamic history—*al-amr bi'l-maruf wa an-nahy an al-munkar* ("commanding right and forbidding wrong")—and detached it from the Holy Law. This commandment in one shape or another appears eight times in the Qur'an.[44] For modern Islamic militants, it is the war cry and justification for the morals police in Saudi Arabia, Iran, the Taliban's Afghanistan, and the neighborhood bands of young men who harass "improperly" attired Muslim women in Baghdad and Marseille. Rarely have Muslim progressives tried to invert this doctrine, which has always been understood in Islamic history as a check on the corrupting, restive, and libidinous side of the human soul, into a defense of political liberty. Although by no means liberals, Sistani and the "traditional" clergy allied with him are turning this doctrine into a pillar of a new, clerically protected democratic order. When I asked Izz ad-Din whether he, his father Grand Ayatollah al-Hakim, Sistani, and the clerical community behind them considered democracy to be *maruf* ["that which is good"], he answered, "Completely. Muslims are entitled to live in a democratic society. Muslims, be they good ones or bad, have the right to vote."[45]

Of course, Izz ad-Din was certain that "good Muslims" would prove triumphant at the ballot box. He had no doubt that Saddam Hussein's tyranny had turned Iraq into a more-religious country. And you cannot spend long with Shiite clerics in Iraq and not smack into the words *khutut hamra*, "red lines," the outer bounds of what is permissible behavior in a democracy. In Iraq today, clerics are often vague about how they see democracy intersecting with the *Shari'a*. They are not, however, practicing *taqiyya*, the age-old Shiite habit of dissimulation before strangers and the powerful. They are just trying to figure out the interplay for themselves after acknowledging one man, one vote as the first and final arbiter of political passions. Iraq's "traditional" clergy knows it is going into uncharted territory. When the mechanics of democratic transition work themselves out, the ulama will no doubt become anxious about "anti-Islamic" and "anti-Shiite" measures in a permanent constitution. But what is striking about the clerical discussion of democratic "red lines" is that it is very difficult for clerics, individually or as a group, to decide what these limits are. In trying to describe these lines, clerics always say that the divisive issues will be about *akhlaq*, "morals," but they are not at all sure which morals should not be open to public debate.

As a historical parallel, in the first half of the nineteenth century, both Shiite and Sunni clerics found imperial Great Britain's aggressive opposition to slavery to be morally absurd and offensive. God via the Qur'an had vouchsafed to believers the right, with detailed restrictions laid out in the Holy Law, to enslave other men and women conquered in war or raiding parties.[46] Slave soldiers had been a proud, critical, and enormously successful part of Islam's military identity for centuries (Cairo's Mamluks and Istanbul's Janissaries are the most famous of these warrior elites). However, Muslim thought evolved, even when British warships were not present to encourage such evolution. Islamic modernists took the lead, but the traditional clergy eventually followed, in declaring enslavement incompatible with Islam. Some Saudis, Sudanese, and Mauritanians may still dream of enslaving nonbelievers, but it is a good bet that most Muslims now find slavery an unacceptable institution, despite its sacrosanct past. Modern sensibilities trumped the Holy Law (the faithful might say times allowed the believer to implement the Qur'an's bias in favor of freedom). Western ideas, including democracy, have been running inside the Muslim intellectual bloodstream since Napoleon conquered Egypt in 1798, nine years before the British unilaterally declared the slave trade an international crime.[47] The seriousness of the discussion about democracy, both in favor and against, increased with time, as more and more Muslims have been exposed to and attracted by Western ways. Socialism, national socialism, and communism all had their day in the Middle East. Democracy, the oldest Western political ideal and perhaps the most alluring (especially after being battered by other Western ideas that expanded the tyrannical capacity of the state), is now an inextricable part of the cultural, if not political, conversation in the Muslim Middle East and the influential Arabic press published in Europe.

Observers unfamiliar with Islamic jurisprudence's concern about minutia and legal consistency (Islamic law is here very similar to the Jewish Talmudic tradition) can easily turn from Sistani's website (www.Sistani.org) certain that the grand ayatollah and his kind are indeed dogmatic medievalists, hopelessly incapable of aiding the birth of a modern democratic state. To the Western observer, it seems oxymoronic to believe that a religious "scholar" who writes about whether a man may eat an animal with which he has had sexual intercourse can be a force for representative government. In a clerical context, however, the two positions do not contradict. Discussing dietary restrictions or the sartorial liberties of single or married observant females, Shiites fall into legal categories where Holy Law prescriptions have not (yet) collided with political experience and great philosophical debate.

This is exactly why Sistani's fatwa and the Iraqi clerical discussion of democracy are so promising: They have decisively broken with the clerical attitude and tradition that on nonpolitical questions seem little changed over the centuries. The only political item that I could find quick agreement on among the "traditional" clergy was that the Qur'an, and the Traditions of the Prophet (the Hadith) and Imam Ali should serve as sources for constitutional and parliamentary law. The traditionalists, however, do not see the Holy Law as *the* source for future legislation. As is the case with Iran's progressive (and still powerless) clerics, what was striking about Iraq's mainline ulama was their philosophical and legal eclecticism. "Neither the Western nor the Islamic traditions are all good or all bad. In each there is something to be used," Sheikh Haqqani stated simply. By contrast, among the clerical followers of the Da'wa Party and the *Sadriyyin*, it is hard to find clerics who want to accept anything that is not divinely inspired. Shaykh Halim al-Fatlawi, a thirty-five-year-old cleric at the al-Hikm mosque in Baghdad's "Sadr City," concisely summed up the difference between the militants and moderates. "They [the moderates] think Iran has got better under Khatami [the reform-minded president of Iran]. I think the early years of Iran were its best."[48]

In the large gray area surrounding the "red lines" lies both tolerance and political pluralism among the clergy and by extension the Shiite community in Iraq. Without tolerance, the agreement to disagree within certain borders, democracy is impossible. By definition, monotheism has a strong antidemocratic current. And Islam's marriage of religion and state into a public praxis was far more successful than in either Christianity or Judaism. But a democratic ethic has been absorbed into the Shiite body politic. They have seen the future thanks to Khomeini, who simply cast aside the Holy Law to construct an Islamic state under his dominion. In his personal quest to create more-perfect believers, he forcibly evolved all Shiites. He demolished the legitimacy (though not the fact) of clerical rule, closing down philosophically one path from Iran's 1905–11 revolution. Left standing, however, is the other pillar: the belief that each citizen has an inalienable right to approve his country's political system. (Khomeini submitted the idea of an Islamic republic to an up-down popular vote in 1979, and regular elections with some element of competition are morally essential to the regime's conception of its own legitimacy, something not at all the case with President Hosni Mubarak's dictatorship in Egypt.)

Sistani and the clerics of Najaf are now building on Khomeini's unintended accomplishment, advancing further the idea that each Muslim has the right to determine the nature of the government over him. Saddam Hussein's Orwellian nightmare no doubt propelled them faster in this direction. The old doctrine of infallible consensus, in Arabic *ijma'*—which in traditional jurisprudence always meant the consensus of qualified legal scholars of a given generation—has now been democratized. God must now share legal sovereignty with man. Clerics must share their ethical monopoly with the ballot box. In traditional Islam, there has always been an understanding that Muslims as a community had a certain moral integrity that stemmed from their direct communication with Allah. Hence, the Tradition of the Prophet that says, "My community will never agree on an error." The believers' acceptance of the Qur'an as the Word of God, the Hadith, and the juridical reasoning of Islam's great legal scholars ultimately depended on a recognition by all that Muslims, as independent, rational actors, could voluntarily see the truth in Islam and its superiority over other callings.

Highly Westernized Muslim liberals and Islamic modernists— faithful Muslims who want to marry the genius of Western innovation with Islamic traditions and values—have always dreamed of expanding the idea of *ijma'* into an argument for democracy. In their hands, it never quite worked, since they saw themselves and were seen by others as outside the Muslim mainstream. This is not true for Sistani and the clerics of Najaf, who are the mainstay of tradition. If Sistani, Grand Ayatollah al-Hakim, and the traditional clergy can keep the hard-core radicals like the *Sadriyyin* in check, it will become increasingly difficult for other Shiite forces in the future, most worrisome Shiite generals commanding a majority Shiite army, to betray a democratic system backed by the most esteemed voices in the community. Contrary to what is commonly believed, secular Shiites, not religiously oriented ones, are probably the most serious long-term threat to the development of a viable democratic system in Iraq.

The traditional clerics are aware of the stakes at home and abroad. "We need the Americans, but the Americans need us. Democracy in the Middle East will not be possible without us," quietly intoned Sayyid Ali al-Wa'iz, a senior Shiite cleric of Baghdad's Kadhimayn shrine, one of the holiest in Iraq. Dressed in white, weak, if not dying, from twenty-three years of detention, the son and grandson of grand ayatollahs, al-Wa'iz smiled softly as he tried to sit up in his bed. "We don't want to repeat the revolution of 1920 [when Shiite clerics rose against the British occupation]. We want democracy this time and we want the coalition troops to go home safely." Not at all annoyed by my repeated questions about the possibility of Shiite militancy gaining the upper hand in Iraq, al-Wa'iz mildly reproved me. "We are all agents of Sistani, who is our *marja* [the "source of emulation," the highest rank for a Shiite cleric]. He is a rational religious scholar. He wants us to live religious lives, but not have religion dictate politics. We must have democracy, not revolution, in Iraq."[49]

The Sunnis

So, is there a Sunni parallel to the political evolution among the Shiites? Inside Iraq, it is easy to find Arab Sunnis who want to see democracy triumph. If for no other reason, fear of a Shiite dictatorship appears to inspire a certain Sunni willingness to embrace some kind of a democratic order. As-Sayyid Jasim Kanas, a devout Sunni elder of the town of Samarra, encapsulated well a "Sunni view" of representative government. For Kanas, democracy would meld together Arabism, Islam, personal security, and the popular will necessary to sustain the enormous reconstruction necessary to recover from the tyranny of Saddam Hussein. "Religion is for God," he intoned, "but government ought to be for *all* the people."[50]

Given the widespread Sunni-led violence in Iraq, particularly among the hard-core *takfiri* fundamentalists, we can lose sight of the fact that the Sunnis will still likely follow the Shiite lead, however reluctantly. Even though the Arab Sunni identity has long been wedded to the idea of political domination—Sunnis have ruled Iraq since the foundation of the Hashemite monarchy in 1921; the Ottoman understanding that Mesopotamia is Sunni territory goes back centuries—Arab Sunnis today realize they are vastly outnumbered by "the other side." The momentum in Iraqi society has now clearly shifted to the Shiites. Badly battered by Sadr and probably not particularly esteemed by Prime Minister Allawi, Grand Ayatollah Sistani can still nonetheless claim de facto veto power over actions by Iraq's unelected government and the American embassy. (For example, even if Allawi had wanted to, he could not have countermanded Sistani's negotiations and deal with Sadr over Najaf in August 2004.) Even if Sistani dies, the *Hawza* will remain a more influential force than any association of Sunni clerics. And both Arab Sunnis and Shiites regularly remark about the lack of revenge killing since the fall of Saddam Hussein even though the pursuit of revenge (*intiqam*) for perceived wrongs is a leitmotif of Iraqi Arab culture. For Ambassador Horan, who knew Iraq since the mid-1950s, the lack of *intiqam* was "astonishing."[51] Culturally, the two communities are very close. Intermarriage is not uncommon. Geographically, the two are dispersed. Iraq's second city, Basra, located deep in the Shiite south, has a population which is probably about one quarter Sunni. Baghdad, which the Sunnis think of as their own, is now probably majority Shiite, perhaps decisively so. Neighborhoods are often mixed. It is most unlikely the Arab Sunni community in Iraq will want to tempt civil war and stand against the Shia.

But democracy in the Middle East obviously does not rise or fall on the participation of Iraqi Sunnis. The principal question is then whether Sunni Islam writ large is able to embrace a democratic ethic? Democracy could triumph in Iraq because the Iraqi Shiite community wills it, but if representative government does not spread to the Sunni nation-states, where 85 to 90 percent of all Muslims live, then the nexus between dictatorship and Islamic extremism is little changed. Bin Ladenism, after all, is a Sunni phenomenon. So could democracy in Iraq spur the growth of representative government elsewhere in the Muslim world? More important, is there a broad parallel in the political experience of Shiites and Sunnis? Since Sunni fundamentalism is the dominant social force in much of the Middle East, could democracy survive a fundamentalist victory at the ballot box?

Sunni Muslim political thought has changed enormously in modern times, which bulldozed the Middle East almost beyond recognition. For centuries, the dominant idea running through Muslim thinking about the nature of legitimate government is probably best expressed by the famous eighth-century jurist, Abu Yusuf: "Fear God and obey him; and if a flat-nosed shrunken-headed Abyssinian slave is invested with power over you, hearken to him and obey him."[52] These same words, which are by some Muslim scholars attributed directly to the Prophet Muhammad, are used again by Islam's greatest medieval theologian, al-Ghazali (d. 1111), to justify obedience to military rulers. There is little doubt that today's unelected rulers in the Middle East are sympathetic to Yusuf's dictum on political legitimacy.

Contemporary Islamic fundamentalists, of course, take issue with this quietist approach. For them, the great hero and intellectual mentor is the jurist Ibn Taymiyya (1263–1328), who declared a holy war against the Mongol lords who had converted to Islam but failed to uphold the Muslim Holy Law. Taymiyya is the intellectual loadstone of the Hanbalite school of religious law, Sunni Islam's youngest and most severe code of conduct. The most extreme practitioners of this school are the Wahhabis, the religious backbone of the modern Saudi state. Despite significant differences among fundamentalists from Morocco to Indonesia, they are united intellectually by certain themes and thinkers. In response to the West's modern superiority over the Islamic world, which became undeniably evident after the waning of the Ottoman empire in the late seventeenth century and Napoleon's easy conquest of Egypt a century later, Muslims seriously started searching for the roots of their weakness and Westerners' strength. Islamic modernists, the most influential belonging to what became known as the Salafi movement, tried to marry European practices, including more representative government, and Western curiosity and innovation to the formative ethos present at Islam's founding. It did not work. The modernists were too obviously adopting Western practices and standards. The very idea of innovation, in Arabic *bid'a*, is synonymous with heresy. Muslim scholasticism, the sclerotic remnant of Islam's once vibrant, creative, and competitive schools of religious thought, hung on in Sunni Islam's madrasas.

But on the fringes of the old system, often fertilized in new Western-oriented schools, modern fundamentalism grew. Under the guidance of such men as the Egyptian Hasan al-Banna, the founder in 1928 of the Muslim Brotherhood; his more intellectual, elitist, and revolutionary disciple, Sayyid Qutb; and Abu al-A'la Mawdudi, a child of Britain's late Indian empire who became perhaps fundamentalism's most disciplined thinker, modern Sunni

Islamic militancy took shape. Like the Salafis, fundamentalists look back at the early Muslim community in Arabia as the ideal. Unlike them but like traditional Sunni Muslim scholars, they see an unchanging Holy Law as eternally valid and capable of being applied to any modern conundrum. They transform the historical, Qur'anic conception of *jahiliyya* (the "age of ignorance" that preceded Muhammad's first revelation) into a timeless term of opprobrium that can be hurled at contemporary Muslims who refuse to strive to re-create the ideal Muslim community. Muslim intellectuals who are guilty of "imported ideas" are the worst sinners. It is a straight and short line from these views to the radical holy warriors who went berserk, slicing the throats and pregnant bellies of "impure" Muslim women in Algeria after the military regime canceled the electoral triumph of the Islamic Salvation Front in 1991. These jihadists are part of the "*takfir*" movement. *Takfir* means "to declare someone an infidel." And infidels, among these men, are subject to death. Osama bin Laden's al Qaeda grew from and grafted onto the *takfiris*, especially those who came with Ayman az-Zawahiri from Egypt's Islamic Jihad Organization.

The intellectual connections are undeniable between "mainstream" Islamic fundamentalism, which grew from al-Banna's Muslim Brotherhood and Mawdudi's Jama'at-i Islami, founded in 1941, and the holy warriors who struck us on 9/11. This is not to suggest, however, that all fundamentalists approved of bin Laden's terrorist attacks. Many Islamic activists condemned the terrorism. But the common roots allow us to see, in part, why bin Laden became and remains a cult figure throughout much of the Muslim world. More important, they allow us to understand how bin Ladenism must be fought—from the inside out. The liberal and neoconservative hope that Muslim moderates or liberal secularists can compete with and vanquish mainstream fundamentalism, which ultimately is the wellhead for bin Ladenism, in a Western context, is to imagine Thomas Jefferson without Martin Luther. In the nineteenth and the twentieth centuries, such progressives repeatedly lost because they ran too far ahead of the mores and sentiments of their societies. And, as important, they were intellectually and politically too derivative of Christians (Europeans), the age-old foes who had more recently conquered much of the Middle East.

Today, nowhere in the Sunni Arab world is fundamentalism intellectually in retreat. Indeed, in Egypt, which is as always the make-or-break country in the Arab world, the appeal and reach of fundamentalism continues to grow, replacing or diluting the country's once dominant secular culture. The urbane and eloquent Egyptian ambassador to the United States, Nabil Fahmy, argues that bin Ladenism is a fringe movement in the Muslim Middle East and especially in his own homeland. He does not see a nexus between the nature of Hosni Mubarak's "presidency" and Islamic extremism.[53] Yet a visit to Cairo's central book market, where fundamentalist literature is stacked everywhere, is too see how completely it dominates pan-Arabism, other non-Islamic nationalist creeds, and Western-style liberalism. By the way, it is not hard to find classics of Western thought translated into Arabic in Egypt, but the market for them is miniscule compared to the appetite for fundamentalist critiques of the West or Qur'anic commentaries.

The American journalist Geneive Abdo, the author of *No God but God: Egypt and the Triumph of Islam*, is perhaps the best street-level reporter on Islamic militancy in Egypt.[54] She chronicles how women of the middle and upper classes, the most natural constituency for progressive politics, are increasingly adopting more traditional clothing and fundamentalist vocabulary and manners. Twenty-five years ago, a visitor to Cairo's American University campus would not have found the often stunningly beautiful daughters of the Egyptian elite veiled. Today, veiled women are everywhere. Clothing in Muslim societies has always been an excellent cultural and political barometer. The Iranian army accepts Western military dress because the accomplishments and allure of Western military power are unchallengeable if not magical. The tie and flesh-exposing dresses, however, are rejected. The former is an unnecessary and fairly recent intrusion of demeaning Occidental tastes. The latter strikes at very old, politically charged Muslim conceptions of prudery and the moral-sexual chemistry undergirding the home, where even the lowliest Muslim male may hope to find an ordered world, pride, and perhaps some bliss. In Egypt, the veil among the American University crowd is a polite but fairly blatant and unpunishable way of signaling one's distance from the improper, if not immoral, secular ethics of the Mubarak regime and the country's modern history.

Abdo echoes the liberal dissident Sa'ad ed-Din Ibrahim: There is a convergence of Muslim fundamentalists, "Islamic democrats," and secularists on the necessity of having a democratically elected alternative to the continuation of dictatorship after the death of President Mubarak (who is seventy-six years old and in spotty health). Abdo believes there is now a "moderate Islamic movement that has softened, parted ways with the Old Guard running the Muslim Brotherhood, and understands it must include diverse views and interests if it expects to gain the trust of Egyptians who in the end will decide if Islamists can be trusted one day to lead the country."[55]

Now, whether Abdo is right about the growth and strength of "Islamic democrats" in Egypt is beside the point. The United States ought to be in favor of Sunni Muslim fundamentalists competing in elections even if we are not sure of their ethics. We should not make the same mistake that the United States and especially France made in Algeria in 1991, when both countries tacitly supported the Algerian military's decision to annul the election results and crack down on Islamist political parties. Assistant Secretary of State for the Near East Edward Djerejian's famous defense of the first Bush administration's fear of Islamic extremism—"one man, one vote, one time"—defined clearly Washington's discomfort with the possibility that free elections could empower Muslim fundamentalists, who could be zealously anti-American and ultimately antidemocratic.[56] Given this choice, a more-or-less pro-American dictatorship was preferable. This decision had widespread support on the Left and Right in the United States and Europe. Feminists applauded the choice. Implicit in the Bush administration's decision was the belief that the dictatorial regimes we supported, no matter how unpleasant, were more likely to evolve politically in a direction we wanted than elected fundamentalists who did not really believe in democracy.

But it ought to be clear now that Washington's calculations thirteen years ago were wrong. The Algerian dictatorship started in 1962, when the French departed. Personalities and parties have changed: The civilian component in the ruling elite has diminished, and the role and influence of the military has increased. The openness of Algerian politics—and they were never open even in the early halcyon days after the country's hard-won independence— only got worse. The bloodlust, which exploded during and after the country's brutal war against France and French Algerians, and which never really attenuated in a postrevolutionary "civil society," resurfaced with a vengeance after 1991. Algeria's generals banned fundamentalist parties from participating in elections, which now occur with little enthusiasm or influence over the military, which continues to rule behind the scenes. And al Qaeda grafted onto the radical Algerian networks in Western Europe, which originally formed to support Islamic militants in North Africa. The rise and lethality of al Qaeda in Europe, which was the all-critical launching platform for 9/11 and probably still harbors the Islamic terrorists operationally most capable of attacking the American mainland, would have been more difficult without Algerian holy warriors and the North African networks they helped construct. A FIS electoral triumph in 1991 might have diverted the passion and energies of the Algerian Islamist expatriates, Muslim Frenchmen, and other North African Arab militants who in the mid- to late 1990s embraced increasingly radical causes.

Compare Algeria with the Islamic Republic of Iran. Even though Iran's ruling clergy has so far successfully thwarted the growth of democracy, it has not stopped the growth of a democratic culture. Ali Khameneh'i and Ali Akbar Hashemi Rafsanjani, the real clerical powers in Tehran, certainly knew in 1997 when Mohammad Khatami won the presidency with 69 percent of the vote on a reform platform that he enjoined far greater political legitimacy in the eyes of the people than they did. The ruling clergy are aware—the reformist press when not shut down constantly reminds it—that free elections are the only basis for legitimate authority in the Islamic Republic. In 1979, however, revolutionary Iran had a holy-war culture among young men. The charismatic Khomeini was truly beloved as the Imam. Many Iranian feminists wrapped themselves in the veil. "Death to America" was the unofficial national anthem.

Twenty-six years after the fall of the shah, Iran's jihadist culture is finished. The ruling mullahs have certainly not forsaken the use of terrorism as a means of statecraft, but the clerical regime no longer has popular support for its anti-American violence. When Iranian-aided bombers blew the Americans out of Beirut in 1983, Tehran's press openly cheered. When Iranian-aided holy warriors truck-bombed the Americans at Khobar Towers in Saudi Arabia in 1996, newspapers neither rapturously recounted the event nor intimated any Iranian complicity. After 9/11, the Islamic Republic witnessed significant public expressions of grief for the United States. Bernard Hourcade, an intrepid French researcher who has long watched firsthand revolutionary sentiments in Iran, thinks a significant portion of the Revolutionary Guards Corps, the muscle of the clerical elite, voted for Khatami in 1997 and 2001.[57] Even the Guard Corps know the old order must have popular legitimacy to survive.

Anti-Americanism is the common denominator of the Arab states with "pro-American" dictators. By comparison, Iran is a profoundly pro-American country. Although it is undoubtedly true that the killing fields of the Iran-Iraq war eventually gutted the holy-war spirit among young Iranian men, the magnetism of martyrdom that was common among male youth until 1986–87 probably prolonged the appeal of Iran's Islamic regime. The young focused on the fraternity of combat and death, not on the incompetence of theocratic government, which started en masse after the war's end in 1988.

If the Islamic Salvation Front had won national power in 1991, then the deconstruction of its most simplistic fundamentalist ideology ("Islam has all the answers") would have begun in earnest. For better or worse, Muslims would have become responsible for their own fate, the essential step in breaking the 9/11 nexus and the noxious conspiracy theories that poison Muslim political and civic culture from Morocco to Pakistan. One would not wish the black years of Iran's Islamic revolution on anyone, but the fear of another Islamic revolution has helped stultify political reform in the Middle East and America's thinking about the reformation of Islamic fundamentalist thought. And there are many reasons to believe that this evolution among Sunni fundamentalists would have been less bloody and convulsive than was the case in Iran. Probably only a small slice of Sunni fundamentalists are *takfiris*; that is, they believe that it is possible that most Muslims could be "bad" Muslims. These are "Pol Pot militants." Even the old guard of the Muslim Brotherhood does not fit this description.

The Sunni Muslim belief in community, in the moral integrity of Muslims as a people, which is scripturally sanctified in the Tradition about Muslims not being capable of agreeing on an error is enormously strong. It would be difficult for Islamic political parties who gain power via the ballot box to dispense with elections. This is probably the principal reason why hard-core Islamists have always dreamed of a coup d'état, of seizing the state as Khomeini did, from the top down. To take it from the bottom up democratically introduces the idea that each Muslim is a rational actor, capable of ascertaining the truth for himself. This conception is not at all foreign to Islamic history and will likely be a philosophical pillar of a new democratic tradition within Muslim societies.

Also, Sunni Muslims have no priesthood, a vanguard of philosopher-kings, to whom they naturally give deference. As Bernard Lewis wrote, "There is no papacy in [traditional] Islam, and there are no equivalents in Muslim history to cardinals Wolsey or Richelieu, Mazarin, or Alberoni."[58] For the Sunnis, there can be no Khomeini. Even among the *takfiris*, there is nervous scavenging of the Qur'an, the Traditions, and scholarly commentary on religious texts to find luminaries whose views might help the revolutionary cause. Disagreement among the hard core, let alone more moderate activists, is common. This populist, protestant impulse is especially powerful among Sunni fundamentalists who grew up in opposition to the established religious hierarchy, which more often than not has been subservient to sultans, kings, and presidents-for-life. The Islamic Salvation Front (FIS) in Algeria had a fourteen-man executive, among whom there were truly frightening ideologues who hated the "imported" idea of democracy as an insult to God's Holy Law.[59] But the front was not a monolith. Ali ibn Hajj, a real fire-breather among the FIS, constantly referred to democracy as "poison" in part because the idea had considerable appeal among the Algerian people, including within Islamic political parties. (The abundant Islamist press at the time makes this crystal clear.[60]) Ibn Hajj, more often called Belhaj, the number two man in FIS, whose views on democracy were well known, nevertheless affixed his name to a public letter to Algeria's military calling for democracy.[61] The declaration juxtaposed the Prophet and his companions with Voltaire, Jefferson, and Thoreau. Belhaj probably knew he could not afford to completely alienate the Algerians, both secular and religious, who wanted a democratic alternative to dictatorship. If the Algerian military had not aborted the democratic process in 1991, elections inevitably would have served as the referee among contending fundamentalists

In Egypt, where the fundamentalist movement is much older, varied, and the culture is less violent, a democratic alternative to the Mubarak regime is constantly discussed.[62] Even if many Egyptians believe change will be slow in coming and the state cannot be violently overturned, certainly a substantial number of Egyptians, perhaps even a majority within the elite, appear to find the current political system corrupt and unsustainable. Egyptians, who are an open people, addicted to movies, magazines, and the outside world, have watched the awful bloodshed in Algeria, the horrific *takfir* violence of homegrown militants who slaughtered foreigners like cattle, and the revolution and reform movement in Iran. Despite the go-slow approach of Mubarak's opposition, worldly Egypt is probably the Arab country that has the best chance of quickly marrying fundamentalism and democracy.

It is certainly possible that fundamentalists, if they gained power in Egypt, would try to end representative government. The democratic ethic, although much more common in Egypt than many Westerners believe, is not as well anchored as it is among the Shiites of Iran or in the fatwas of Grand Ayatollah Sistani. But the United States would still be better off with this alternative than with a secular dictatorship, like Mubarak's, which oppresses and feeds fundamentalism. Without Mubarak or the general who is likely to succeed him, evolution starts. The Iranian model comes into play. Fundamentalists become fundamentalist critics. They become responsible for their own spiritual destiny, in addition to potholes, sewage pipes, imports, exports, and the nation's credit rating. The State Department talks about encouraging "generational" change. But time moves quickly now. Given how rapidly bin Ladenism went from an idea to an operational reality, we are of course lucky this is so. In twenty years, the Iranian revolution collapsed and the clerical regime, not the United States, became the principal focus of the people's anger. The same process is unavoidable in Egypt and elsewhere in the Muslim world, if Islamic activists become dictators or elected representatives wielding real power.

And the reverberations of a democratic success in Iraq could be large. Sistani's arguments and actions in favor of democracy are likely to have more traction in the Sunni world than Khomeini's revolutionary call. Iraq's grand ayatollahs and democrats use Arabic, not Persian. Thinking of Iraq's Sunni Arabs and Kurds, and probably of the Sunni Arab world beyond, Sistani and the senior clerics of Najaf have studiously avoided using Shiite religious allusions that so angered Sunni fundamentalists in the past. Sistani and Grand Ayatollah al-Hakim, Najaf's number two, are modest, unpretentious men who make arguments for one man, one vote in clear, simple Arabic. They can be understood by even the least educated.

And, if Iraq progresses, shame among the Sunnis could well come into play. If lowly and long-belittled Muslims can establish a functioning democracy, why can't we? And the trial of Saddam Hussein, which now seems too far off to even imagine, will likely be riveting television.[63] Even the Arab satellite networks—and all Arabic satellite TV channels in the Middle East, save the Lebanese Hizbollah's, are anti-Shiite—will have an enormously difficult time hiding the horrors of Saddam's rule. Many in the Arab world will surely see images of a dictator and police-state tactics that have things in common with regimes closer to home. And looking east toward Iran, the evolution of an Iraqi democracy protected by the Iraqi clergy will not be greeted happily in Tehran. Intra-Shiite squabbles do matter, and this one between clerics who believe in one man, one vote and those who believe in theocracy is an enormous difference of opinion. We should not be fooled by the publicly cordial relations that exist between clerics of Najaf and Tehran. Najaf's position on democracy is an explicit negation of Ayatollah Khameneh'i's right to rule.

Nonetheless, the march of democracy in the Middle East is likely to be *very* anti-American. Decades of American support to Middle Eastern dictators helped create bin Ladenism. Popular anger at Washington's past actions may not fade quickly, even if the United States were to switch sides and defend openly all the parties calling for representative government. Nationalism and fundamentalism, two complementary forces throughout most of the Middle East, will likely pump up popular patriotism. Such feelings always have a sharp anti-Western edge to them. That is what Professor Lewis called "the clash of civilizations."[64] Fourteen hundred years of tense, competitive history is not easily overcome, but this antagonism can diminish.

No country could have been more anti-American than revolutionary Iran. But, as Iranian political culture has become more democratic and anger at clerical supremacy increased, anti-Americanism has waned. There are bound to be significant differences in the way other Muslim states evolve vis-à-vis the United States, but ultimately democracies share certain values, reflexes, and affinities that make them more secure and comfortable with each other than democracies are with dictatorships. If General

Pervez Musharraf is killed, we do not know what our relationship with Pakistan will be. If the Indian prime minister dies—it is not as easy to recall his name—his death does not really matter. The United States's ever-deepening and friendlier relations with an increasingly democratic and self-critical India will continue. If there is a cure for the competition and confrontation between the West and Islam, Muslim democracies are essential to it.

Which brings us to Israel and other things that Muslims find distasteful. Muslim moderates and liberals usually argue that the United States must solve the Israeli-Palestinian confrontation to improve the chances for democracy in the Muslim Middle East. Like Islamic modernists of yesteryear, they have to protect themselves against charges of dual loyalty since they are so thoroughly Westernized. Their moderation in the fundamentalist press inevitably becomes pro-Zionism, a difficult, sometimes deadly, position politically anywhere in the Arab world. Arab liberals especially often make democracy sound like a beauty contest (American liberals frequently do the same thing[65]): It will win in the Muslim Middle East only if the United States is sufficiently appealing. America's pro-Israeli stance, the wars in Iraq, Abu Ghurayb, or Christian fundamentalism in the heartland, so their theory goes, can make democracy a hard, if not impossible, sell to Muslims.

Democracy-pushing fundamentalists, of course, never make this argument. Neither often do the softer "Islamic democrats" of Geneive Abdo. These people dislike, usually detest, Israel. A "just," "equitable" settlement to them is not Israeli and Palestinian states living happily side by side. Indeed, active American engagement in the peace process makes fundamentalists hate the United States more, not less, because such engagement is premised on Muslims surrendering their God-given historical right to part of the core lands of the *dar al-Islam* ("the House of Islam"), conquered in the seventh century, the golden age of the "rightly guided" caliphs, the most esteemed successors of the Prophet Muhammad. The virtues of democracy for them are not contingent on U.S. actions. Like many Latin American democrats, these Muslims often want democracy to stand tall and united against American influence.

Democracy would reinvigorate Muslim pride, laid low by illegitimate Muslim despots who cater to the United States. Vis-à-vis the Islamists, Muslim moderates and liberals are in a politically unwinnable position since they must control the American political system before they can control their own.

And it is worth stressing again that, even if democracy fails the first time around, it is still the best option for the United States. Islamic fundamentalism must evolve to kill off bin Ladenism. In opposition to "pro-American" dictatorial regimes, there is no historical reason to believe it will. The frustration, anger, and the holy-warrior reflex to target the United States as the power behind the despots can only grow. Middle Eastern observers have often hoped that Arab rulers would eventually evolve into Mustafa Kemal Ataturk, the dictatorial founder of the Turkish republic who laid the groundwork for Turkey's secular democracy. "Kemalism" is common among American scholars, diplomats, and spooks who love the Arab world but appreciate the greater progress and promise of the Turks. This, too, has been an Israeli hope, given the proper, if not friendly, relations that have always existed between the Turkish Republic and the Jewish state (although it is probably accurate to say that most Israelis, like most Jewish Americans, have been dismissive of Muslim civil rights).

It ought to be clear, however, that the Arab world is too historically and culturally different from Turkey to produce an Ataturk. The Ottoman empire was intimately intertwined with Europe for centuries. No Arab ruler can say what Ataturk said easily.

> Our thoughts, our mentality, are going to be civilized [that is, to be made European] . . . we're going to be civilized and proud of it. Look at the state of the rest of the . . . Muslims! What catastrophes and disasters have come upon them, because their minds could not adjust themselves to the all-encompassing and sublime dictates of civilization! This is why we too

remained backward for so long, and why we finally plunged into the last morass [the defeat of the Ottoman empire in World War I]. If we have been able to save ourselves in the last few years, it has been because of the change in our mentality. We can never stop again. . . . We can't go back. . . . Civilization is a blazing fire that burns and obliterates those who will not acknowledge her.[66]

The Turks are enormously lucky that the Qur'an was not first uttered in their native language. And Ataturk *was* that rare exception to Lord Acton's dictum about power corrupting. The growth of Turkish democracy, which has become increasingly secure since the more populist and religious stewardship in the 1980s and 1990s of Turgut Özal, has made the Turkish Republic at home and abroad more willing to criticize the United States. Turkey's quest—now advanced vigorously by the ruling Islamist-sympathetic AK party—to join the European Union will likely fortify further this faith-based, anti-American democratic direction. The secular age in the Middle East, which gained speed after World War I, when Muslims threw themselves into socialism, national socialism, and communism, is long gone. It died in 1967, when the Israelis made mincemeat of the "New Arab Man."

Arab dictators and kings are most unlikely freely to pass sovereignty to their people, who would probably judge their ex-rulers and the families and friends of their ex-rulers somewhat harshly. With rare exceptions—King Abdallah of Jordan and his Hashemite family might survive—too much abuse and ill-gotten gains have been doled out. For his family, friends, and their accumulated wealth, Hosni Mubarak is undoubtedly right when he says that democracy in Egypt would mean "chaos."[67]

But the United States really has no alternative to switching its allegiances from the rulers to the ruled. To do otherwise is to run against the growing Muslim belief that political legitimacy can come only from the ballot box. It is also to run against the American democratic ethic, which is the wellspring of our national soul. The

United States should use its bully pulpit and its economic muscle to encourage those who want change and punish those who do not. In doing so, we will undoubtedly aid those who hate us and we may well hurt true friends. We should be generous in opening our borders to those secular Muslims who cannot stomach the democratic transition. Westernized women who grew up under secular dictatorships may find it very rough going. Many Israelis and their American supporters may rise in horror contemplating replacing peace-treaty-signing dictators with fundamentalists who may partly build a democratic consensus on anti-Zionism. But down this uneasy path lies an end to bin Ladenism and the specter of an American city attacked with weapons of mass destruction. Although he certainly did not intend to, Ayatollah Khomeini and his holy warriors illuminated the way. All the other roads lead us back to 9/11.

Notes

1. See Patricia Wilson, "Kerry: Bush 'Chose' Iraq War, Americans Pay Bill," *Reuters*, September 7, 2004; Glenn Kessler, "Kerry: Democracy Can Wait," *Manchester Guardian Weekly*, June 4, 2004; Dan Balz, "Kerry Attacks and Defends," *Boston Globe*, April 19, 2004; David M. Halbfinger, "Kerry Says Bush's Stubbornness Hurts Troops," *Washington Post*, April 15, 2004; Glen Johnson, "Kerry Urges President to Share Responsibility in Iraq," *New York Times*, April 15, 2004.

2. Read William F. Buckley, Jr., for perhaps the most open example of serious, shifting cogitation and anxiety about the war. See his "Should We Have Gone to War?" *National Review Online*, July 13, 2004.

3. For Lewis's fullest explication see his *What Went Wrong: Western Impact and Middle Eastern Response* (New York: Oxford University Press, 2002) and *The Crisis of Islam: Holy War and Unholy Terror* (New York: Modern Library, 2003). Also see his seminal essay, "The Roots of Muslim Rage," *Atlantic Monthly*, September 1990, pp. 47–60. For a very succinct exposition, see Lewis's "Time for Toppling," *Wall Street Journal*, September 27, 2002. For Ajami, see his *The Dream Palace of the Arabs: A Generation's Odyssey* (New York: Pantheon Books, 1998), in particular chapters 3 and 4, "In the Shape of the Ancestors" and "In the Land of Egypt," respectively, pp. 111–253. Also see his "The Sentry's Solitude" in *Foreign Affairs*, November/December 2001, pp. 2–16; and "Iraq and the Arabs' Future," *Foreign Affairs*, January/February 2003, pp. 2–18; and his commentary post-9/11 in *U.S. News and World Report* and the *Wall Street Journal*.

4. Conversation with President Ford at AEI's World Forum, Beaver Creek, Colorado, June 2003.

5. From Samuel P. Huntington, *The Third Wave: Democratization in the Late Twentieth Century* (Norman: University of Oklahoma Press, 1991), pp. 298–99.

6. George W. Bush, "George W. Bush Delivers Remarks on the 20th Anniversary of the National Endowment for Democracy" (speech, Washington, D.C., November 6, 2003). See http://www.whitehouse.gov/news/releases/2003/11/20031106-2.html.

7. See Marina Ottoway and Thomas Carothers, "The Greater Middle East Initiative, Off to a False Start," Policy Brief # 29, March 2004, Carnegie Endowment for International Peace. Also see M. Ottoway, "Avoiding the Women's Rights Trap," *Arab Reform Bulletin*, Carnegie Endowment for Peace, July 2004; and her "Women's Rights and Democracy in the Arab World," Number 42, Carnegie Papers, Middle East Series, February 2004.

8. For more information on the U.S.-Islamic World Forum, see http://www.us-islamicworldforum.org/.

9. William J. Clinton, Closing Address, U.S.–Islamic World Forum, Doha, Qatar, January 10–12, 2004. See http://www.brook.edu/dybdocroot/fp/research/projects/islam/clinton20040112.pdf.

10. Daniel Benjamin and Steven Simon, *The Age of Sacred Terror* (New York: Random House, 2003), p. 415.

11. Senior Democratic staffer, London, January 13, 2004. The senior staffer had doubts about whether Prince Abdallah's discussions reflected a sincere desire within the Saudi family for greater political openness and transparency. Abdallah's actions appeared more linked to President Bush's concerns than royal-family anxiety about the political status quo in Saudi Arabia. This view is supported by the fact that the national Saudi press gave little attention to the Shiite participation in the National Dialogues, much less than the Saudi press aimed or published abroad.

12. "Mubarak Leads 'Rebellion' against Bush Mideast Initiative," *Middle East Online,* February 26, 2004. See www.middle-east-online.com/English/?id+9047 and "French-German Initiative for ME reform," March 6, 2004, on www.Turks.us. See www.turks.us/article.php?story=2004030601560097.

13. See, for example, Amr Moussa's commentary in "It's Pouring Initiatives," *al-Ahram*, February 26, 2004.

14. Neil MacFarquhar, "Summit Collapse Leaves Arab Leaders in Disarray," *New York Times*, March 28, 2004.

15. Richard Clarke, *Against All Enemies* (New York: Free Press, 2004), pp. 245–91.

16. Zbigniew Brzezinski, *The Choice: Global Domination or Global Leadership* (New York: Basic Books, 2004), p. 415.

17. Henry Kissinger, "Selling Democracy," *Baltimore Sun*, April 11, 2004.

18. See Ottoway, "Women's Rights and Democracy in the Arab World."

19. Richard N. Haass, "Toward Greater Democracy in the Muslim World," *Washington Quarterly*, Summer 2003, pp. 137–48.

20. Conversations with Bernard Lewis; see also his commentary in *What Went Wrong*, pp. 70–74, and his *The Middle East: A Brief History of the Last 2,000 Years* (New York: Scribner, 1995), pp. 382–84.

21. See for example Wolfowitz's speech at Georgetown University, October 30, 2003.

22. See for good, detailed commentary on the attacks in France in 1995, Ali Laidi and Ahmad Salam, *Le Jihad en Europe: Les Filières du Terrorisme Islamiste* (Paris: Seuil, 2002), pp. 195–205.

23. The 9/11 Commission Report (New York: W. W. Norton, 2004), pp. 362–63.

24. Kissinger, "Selling Democracy."

25. Jackson Diehl, "Listen to the Arab Reformers," *Washington Post*, March 29, 2004.

26. Sa'ad Eddin Ibrahim, "The Sick Man of the World," *Washington Post*, March 28, 2004.

27. *Arab Human Development Report 2002* (New York: United Nations Publications, 2002).

28. Bush, "George W. Bush Delivers Remarks on the 20th Anniversary of the National Endowment for Democracy."

29. Ambassador Hume Horan, e-mail message to the author, March 6, 2004.

30. Conversation with the author in Paris, July 15, 2004.

31. "Al-Hakim's Brother Speaks at Funeral," *BBC Monitoring Middle East*, September 2, 2003.

32. Ambassador Hume Horan, e-mail message to the author, March 27, 2004.

33. Ibid.

34. Ibid.

35. For a succinct, intimate, and somewhat eclectic history of the Iraqi Shia in the mid-twentieth century, see Pierre-Jean Luizard, *La Question Irakienne* (Paris: Fayard, 2002). See in particular chapters 2 and 3, "Un État construit contre sa société (1921–1958)" and "La République des illusions perdues (1958–1968)," respectively, pp. 35–82. Also see on the Shia and Communism, Graham E. Fuller and Rend Rahim Francke, *The Arab Shi'a: The Forgotten Muslims* (New York: St. Martin's Press, 1999), pp. 87–118.

36. Luizard, *La Formation de L'Irak Contemporain: Le role politique des ulémas chiites à la fin de la domination ottomane et au moment de la creation de l'État irakien* (Paris: Éditions du CNRS, 1991).

37. Conversation with Luizard in Paris, July 16, 2003.

38. Izz ad-Din, conversation with the author, June 12, 2003.

39. Shaykh Muhammad Haqqani, conversation with the author, June 11, 2003.

40. Ibid.

41. Yitzak Nakash, *The Shi'is of Iraq* (Princeton, N.J.: Princeton University Press, 1995), p. 50.

42. Grand Ayatollah Sayyid Ali Husayni Sistani's official website, http://www.Sistani.org, June 30, 2003. Translated from the original by the author.

43. L. Carl Brown, *Religion and State* (New York: Columbia University Press, 2000), p. 172.

44. For a comprehensive study of *al-amr bi'l-maruf*, see Michael Cook's magisterial *Commanding Right and Forbidding Wrong in Islamic Thought* (Cambridge: Cambridge University Press, 2000). This is an unrivaled study of what might be called Islam's "categorical imperative."

45. Izz ad-Din, conversation with the author, June 13, 2003.

46. For a discussion of slavery in the Arab world, see Murray Gordon, *Slavery in the Arab World* (New York: National Book Network, 1989); and Bernard Lewis, *Race and Slavery in the Middle East: An Historical Enquiry* (New York: Oxford University Press, 1990). In particular, see *Race and Slavery*, pp. 78–84.

47. On the penetration of Western ideas into the Muslim world, see Bernard Lewis, *The Muslim Discovery of Europe* (New York: W. W. Norton, 1982, updated 2001), pp. 50–57. Also see for a good, concise discussion of the early Western impact on Muslim thought, Hichem Djaït, "La pensée arabo-musulmane et les Lumières" in *Islam et politique* (Paris: Éditions Gallimard, 1991), pp. 32–52.

48. Shaykh Halim al-Fatlawi, conversation with the author, June 8, 2003.

49. Sayyid Ali al-Wa'iz, conversation with the author, June 15, 2003.

50. As-Sayyid Jasim Kanas, conversation with the author, June 14, 2003.

51. Ambassador Horan, e-mail message to the author, March 27, 2004.

52. Ann K. S. Lambton, *State and Government in Medieval Islam* (Oxford: Oxford University Press, 1981), pp. 56–57.

53. Nabil Fahmy, interview by Vicky O'Hara, *Morning Edition*, NPR, March 23, 2004.

54. Geneive Abdo, *No God but God: Egypt and the Triumph of Islam* (New York: Oxford University Press, 2000).

55. Abdo, "The Other Islamic Revolution," *Boston Globe Magazine*, July 20, 2003.

56. Edward Djerejian, *Developments in the Middle East: Hearing of the Europe and Middle East Subcommittee of the House Foreign Affairs Committee*, 103rd Congress, 1st Session, July 27, 1993.

57. Conversations with Hourcade from 1997 through 2004. Also see his agile analysis in "Quand l'Iran s'éveillera . . ." in *Politique Internationale*, Fall 2003, pp. 177–96.

58. Bernard Lewis, *Islam in History* (Chicago: Open Court Press, 1993), p. 273.

59. For a detailed discussion of the FIS and its evolution, see Ahmed Rouadjia, *Les frères et la mosquée: Enquête sur le mouvement islamiste en Algérie* (Paris: Karthala, 1990).

60. For commentary by Belhaj on democracy, see his articles in *El-Mounquid*, numbers 23 and 24, published in M. Al-Ahnaf, Bernard Botiveau, and Franck Frégosi, *L'Algérie par ses islamistes* (Paris: Karthala, 1991), pp. 87–98.

61. Ibid, pp. 84–103. See also Noah Feldman, *After Jihad: America and the Struggle for Islamic Democracy* (New York: Farrar, Straus and Giroux, 2003), pp. 223–24.

62. See again Abdo's "The Other Islamic Revolution." Also see David Remnick's "Going Nowhere: The Problem with Democracy in Egypt," Letter from Cairo, *The New Yorker*, July 12 and 19, 2004, pp. 74–83. Remnick conveys well the intellectual yeast in Egypt's politics. However, he has a distinctly liberal, America-centric take on Egypt's political future. "Part of the collateral damage of the Bush Administration's prosecution of the war in Iraq is the erosion of American prestige and influence all over the world." Therefore, the attractiveness and force of America's democratic arguments have been weakened in the Middle East. In Remnick's view, the war has spurred the radicalization of Egyptian society and diminished its democratic potential.

63. Unless ex-Baathists behind Prime Minister Allawi are successful in compressing the trial of Saddam for fear that a prolonged reflection on the crimes of the Baath party would be psychologically and politically too disturbing.

64. Bernard Lewis, "Roots of Muslim Rage," *Atlantic Monthly*, September 1990, pp. 47–60.

65. See the author's "Who's Afraid of Abu Ghraib?" *Weekly Standard*, May 24, 2004.

66. Geoffrey Lewis, *Modern Turkey* (New York: Praeger, 1974), pp. 125–26.

67. Neil MacFarquhar, "Arab Leaders Seek to Counter U.S. Plan for Mideast Overhaul," *New York Times*, March 4, 2004.

About the Author

Reuel Marc Gerecht is a resident fellow at the American Enterprise Institute, a contributing editor to *The Weekly Standard*, and a correspondent for *The Atlantic Monthly*. Formerly a Middle Eastern specialist for the Central Intelligence Agency, Mr. Gerecht is the author of *Know Thine Enemy: A Spy's Journey into Revolutionary Iran* (Farrar, Straus and Giroux, 1997) and a contributor to *Present Dangers: Crisis and Opportunity in American Foreign and Defense Policy*, edited by Robert Kagan and William Kristol (Encounter Books, 2000). He has also been a commentator on the Middle East, Shiism, terrorism, and intelligence issues in the *New York Times*, the *Wall Street Journal*, the *Washington Post*, *The New Republic*, *Foreign Affairs*, *Foreign Policy*, and other leading American and international publications. He is a graduate of Johns Hopkins University and Princeton University, where he received his MA in Islamic history.